Bramber Castle

and the Rise and Fall of
the House of Braose

The story of a former baronial castle in West
Sussex, England,
and the noble family who built it

by Michael L. Clark

Cover and Text Design: Michael L. Clark

ISBN: 978-0-9916179-4-4

To Wendy, whose cooperation and forbearance made this book possible.

Table of Contents

Figure 1 - Bramber Castle within England

Preface

This book began in 2018 as a series of YouTube videos for my channel, A Yank in Sussex, not long after I married my English wife, Wendy, to whom this volume is dedicated. The subject of the book is the castle I can see from the backyard of our home in England.

My fascination for all things British has its roots in the time when my father's employment in 1969 took my family to Cheltenham, Gloucestershire in England. I lived there with them for two years until my path in life diverged and I returned to the United States.

I loved England, and I especially loved its history. As I wandered the countryside on my motorcycle (even visiting France with my younger brother during the summer), among the things I discovered were an archaeological dig in the Cotswold Hills above Gloucester, Stonehenge and Avebury Ring in the Salisbury Plain, and castles! The school I attended at the time, called Cheltenham Grammar School, was even designed to look somewhat like a castle, although it was not at all ancient, having been built in the early 1960s, according to a design by its headmaster, Dr. A. E. Bell, whom I greatly admired.

Once I returned to the US, I never expected to find my way back to England again. However, before my dear wife Waltraut passed away in 2015, she insisted that I remarry, and this led to my finding a lovely English widow, and my subsequent joining her in England's "green and pleasant land."

The production of my three videos about Bramber Castle required a good deal of research, and since the material I uncovered was much more extensive than what I could cover in the limited format of my videos, there was a lot that remained unsaid. So, once I published the third and final video, the idea occurred to me of assembling all the things I had learned in order to produce an informative book about the castle. The book you see before you is the result – after a fair amount of procrastination.

A small caution is indicated. While I have tried to be as accurate and as factual as possible, what we're dealing with here is something along the lines of ancient history. Centuries and records have come and gone. And since paper is delicate and subject to loss of many different kinds, some of history has been lost along with it. This will be reflected in the completeness of the information presented.

There are a few places in this book where I will express an opinion that disagrees with the conclusions that men and women of greater expertise have come to. In those instances, I will try to make it clear that I disagree, and give plausible reasons for my disagreement. This doesn't happen often, but I thought I should warn you!

I hope that you find Bramber Castle as interesting as I have!

Michael L. Clark
19 April 2024

Introduction

There are somewhere around 1,500 castles in England and Wales, ranging in condition from barely recognizable ruins to still occupied and functional fortresses. Among the functional and occupied castles is the royal residence known as Windsor Castle, where King Charles III lives when he is not at his one of his other royal residences. This is located just 20 miles west of central London, not far from Heathrow Airport. It is frequently visible from aircraft arriving and departing from the airport, as it sits just to the side of the airport's western flight path. This castle was built by William the Conqueror not long after his conquest of England in 1066, and it is coming up on its thousandth birthday.

The barely recognizable castle remnants include the grass-covered dirt mound which is all that remains of the motte of Chichester Castle, in West Sussex. It was believed to have been built sometime in the 12th century as the administrative headquarters of the westernmost district of Sussex, but as it was never given stone walls, it has not survived in any noteworthy fashion. It's quite unrecognizable as a castle.

Somewhere in between the few fully functional and many barely recognizable examples there is a large number of merely ruined castles (some of them more ruined than others), and one of these, Bramber Castle, is the subject of this book. There isn't much of it left. The most prominent part is the very visible remnant of the gate tower, but one can also see parts of the stone curtain wall, and the stumps of another tower which once overlooked the estuary of the River Adur.

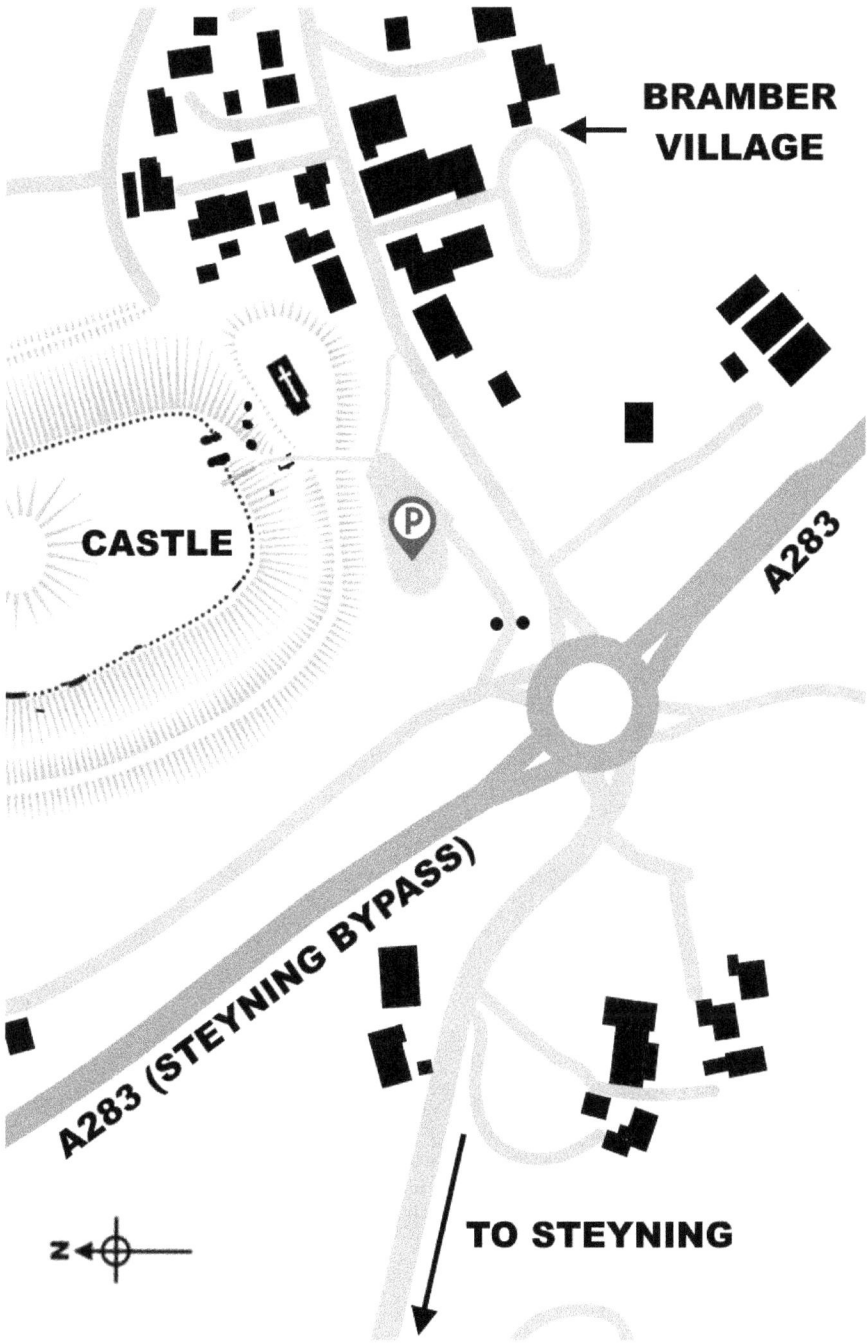

BRAMBER VILLAGE

CASTLE

A283

A283 (STEYNING BYPASS)

TO STEYNING

Z

Figure 2- Map of the local area around Bramber Castle

AERIAL VIEW OF BRAMBER CASTLE (SPRING 2024)

Figure 3

BRAMBER VILLAGE with BRAMBER BROOKS in the foreground (Castle to the right)

Figure 4

5

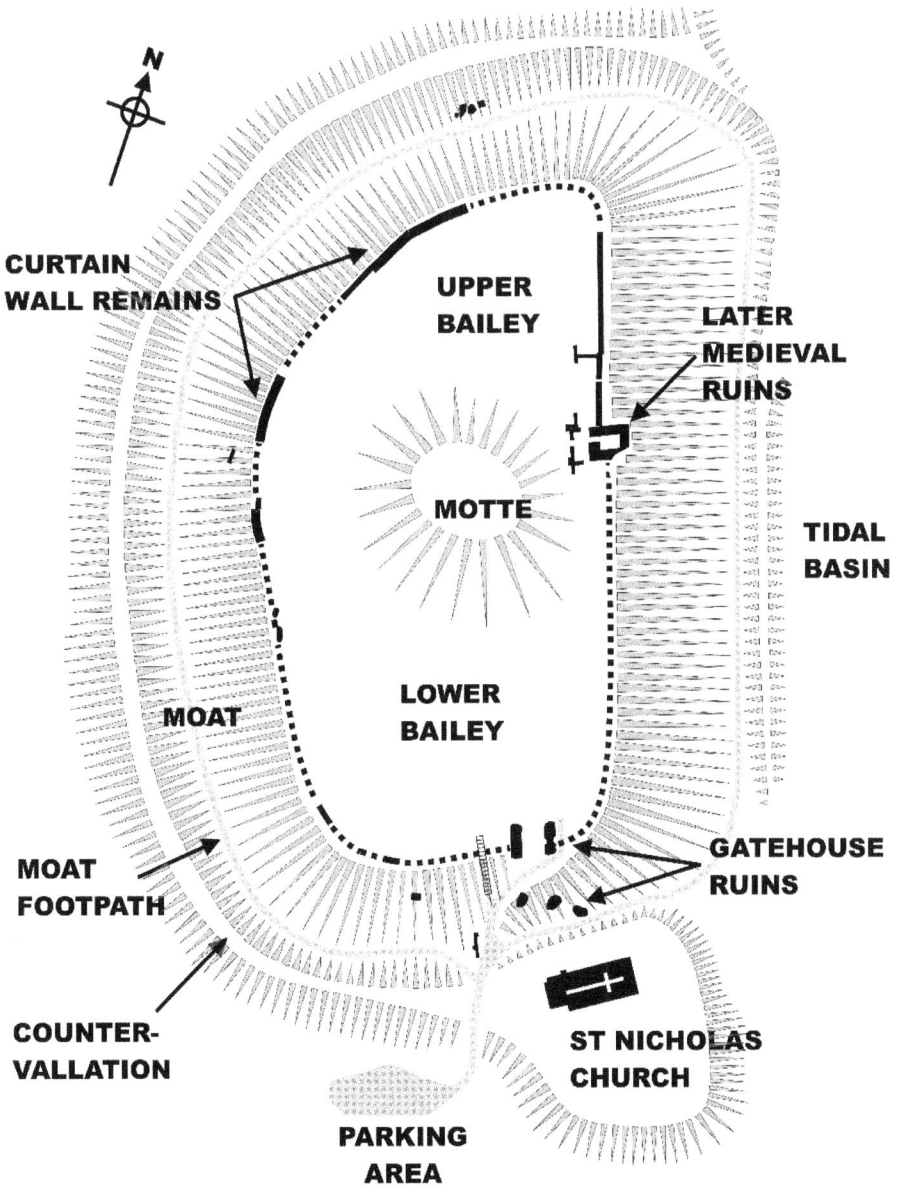

N

CURTAIN
WALL REMAINS

UPPER
BAILEY

LATER
MEDIEVAL
RUINS

MOTTE

TIDAL
BASIN

MOAT

LOWER
BAILEY

MOAT
FOOTPATH

GATEHOUSE
RUINS

COUNTER-
VALLATION

ST NICHOLAS
CHURCH

PARKING
AREA

BRAMBER CASTLE TODAY

Figure 5 – Bramber Castle modern remains

A Walk Around the Castle

Bramber Castle, owned by English Heritage, is located just a mile outside of the town of Steyning in West Sussex, England. The castle sits on a chalk knoll next to the village of the same name. The village grew up around the castle and along the causeway that William de Braose, the castle's founder, built not long after the castle was completed.

The castle is approached from the roundabout along the Steyning Bypass between Steyning and Bramber. One drives up the incline between two decorative castellated mini-towers and onto a rather rough-and-ready gravel road to the parking area. Parking is free, as is entry to the castle, and it's open year-round during daylight hours.

BRAMBER CASTLE SITE ENTRANCE

Figure 6

Below the castle and just opposite the parking lot is the St. Nicholas church. This church is operated by the Church of

England and remains in consecration as an active house of worship. Religious services are held here regularly each Sunday. It was originally built in 1073, around the same time as the castle itself. Its original purpose was to serve as a convenient place of worship for the inhabitants of the castle.

After walking past the church one continues up the gravel path to the castle proper. The first part of the castle one passes by is what remains of the old bridge over the moat. On the left is one of the bridge support walls, with visible holes for bridge deck support joists. On the other side of that support wall is what little remains of the corresponding other half of the bridge support. Where the bridge deck once crossed the moat it is now simply part of the gravel path.

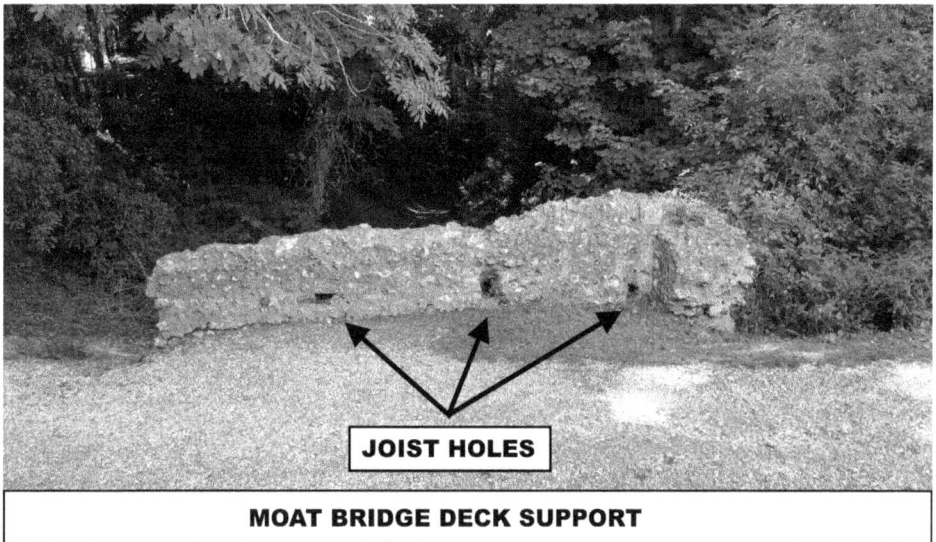

JOIST HOLES

MOAT BRIDGE DECK SUPPORT

Figure 7

While standing where the bridge used to be you can see the castle's moat extending both east and west. The moat extends all around the castle and is up to 75 feet in depth compared to the castle's bailey. The eastward moat heads downwards towards the old River Adur estuary, which is the steepest part of the moat's edge.

The term "bailey," by the way, refers to the high ground on which most of the castle's structures are placed. A bailey (also called a ward) in a fortification is a leveled courtyard, typically enclosed by a curtain wall.

The entire moat is walkable from the bridge. It's roughly level around the south, west, and north sides of the castle, but on the east side it plunges quite steeply to the former estuary. It's still walkable, but the slopes require some care to do so.

MOAT VIEW EASTWARDS FROM BRIDGE

Figure 8

As you look eastwards along the moat you can see three very large chunks of old masonry which have fallen into the moat. They used to be part of the old gate tower, but ground instability, possibly due to deepening of the moat in the 1200s, caused most of the tower to fall into the moat. This didn't happen all at once. Some documentary evidence shows that only the south wall of the tower had fallen by the mid-1600s.

MOAT VIEW WESTWARDS FROM BRIDGE

Figure 9

The only remaining part of the old gate tower, or "keep," are very obvious as you continue up the path. It stands today as the one recognizable evidence that there was once a full castle here.

REMAINS OF THE GATE TOWER AS SEEN FROM THE BRIDGE

Figure 10

This remaining wall of the tower stands about 56 feet or 17 meters above ground level, nearly at its original height. It has one window opening just over halfway up, and on what would have been the interior wall, joist holes are visible at three levels, one of which corresponds to the window opening. East of the tower wall one can see the stump of the west wall.

Figure 11 - East side of gate tower remnant showing floor joist holes

Figure 12 - Gate tower remnant showing intramural opening

On the west side of the tower, besides the window opening there is another opening about one-third of the way up the tower, near a corner. This is what is left of an intramural passage that apparently provided access between the inside of the tower to a part of the original castle wall that is no longer standing. A close look at the passage shows that there is an alcove there, possibly for storage or shelter from the weather.

With a pair of binoculars or a telescopic lens one can see what appears to be some old graffiti scratched on one stone of the wall inside the passage. The graffiti consists of Latin letters and numerals, with the larger and more deeply incised letters being "DJMCH". This inscription may or may not be ancient, and what it signifies is unknown. The other set of letters and numbers are clearly more modern. They consist of the name "EDISON" and the numerals "1891," which are scratched less deeply using smaller letters, above and below "DJMCH."

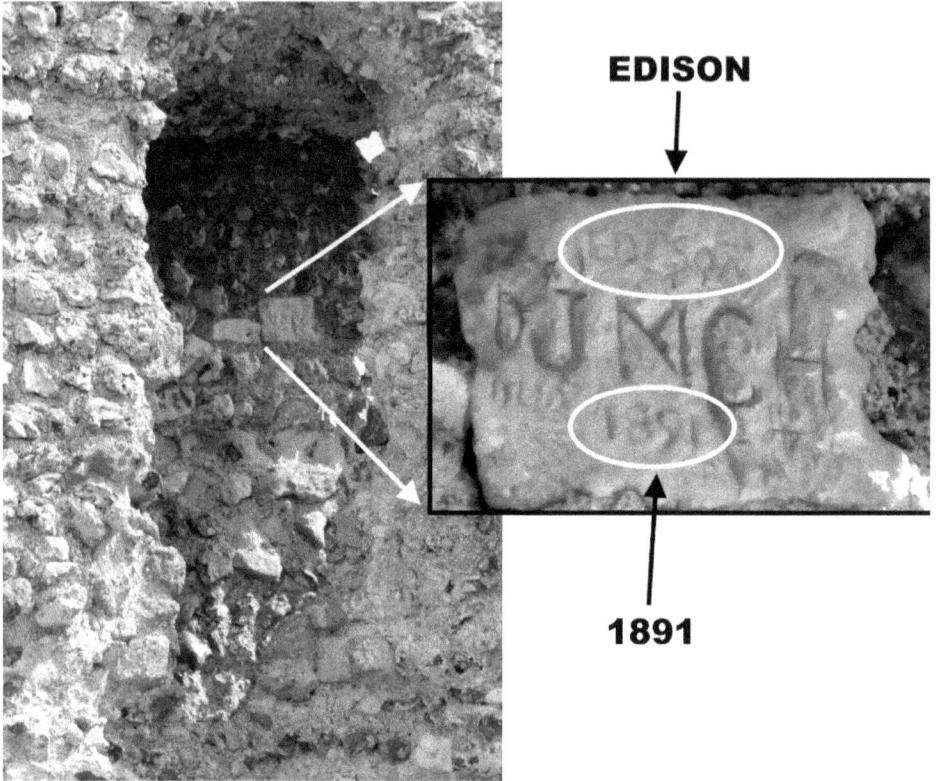

I presume that sometime in 1891 an adventurer named Edison climbed to the intramural opening in order to leave evidence of his daring where it would be sure to be noticed by generations of visitors to come. Perhaps by placing the evidence in a somewhat obscure place, he (and I presume it was a "he") by his subtlety ensured only the most observant would discover it.

Turning from the remains of the gate tower, directly in front of us, dominating the center of view, is a large, tree-covered mound, which, in castle-speak is called the "motte." This earthen mound rises to a height of some 30 feet (10 meters). The motte is the part of the castle which was designed as the place for final defense against attack, and would normally feature a stone fortification, called a "keep," at its summit. This motte, however, is bare of any structure.

THE MOTTE

Figure 13

On one of my visits to the castle I ascended to the motte's summit, where I found there were no trees at the very top. In the grass there I did see, however, a circular and bare indentation that seems to have been used to contain a small fire. Perhaps someone in the recent past felt inclined to camp up there one night. Which would have been entirely against the rules of course!

THE SUMMIT OF THE MOTTE

Figure 14

Returning to the castle's bailey, as we continue on our walk, moving to the left around the castle's perimeter after our ascent of the path to the bailey, we can see a number of segments of the old curtain wall. The first one is quite obscure! This is because it's hidden by a tree. But it's not just behind a tree; the tree's roots cover it!

At intervals further along the perimeter we encounter the rest of the remaining wall. Some parts are just a few feet or a meter or so high, but others rise up to ten feet or three meters.

Finally, after we've gone three-quarters of the way around the motte, we find what is labelled on the English Heritage informational panels as "Later Medieval Ruins." This

CURTAIN WALL REMNANTS

A PART OF THE CURTAIN WALL ENCASED IN TREE ROOTS

Figure 15

seems to have included the base of a tower built at the bailey's edge, as well as rooms used for utility functions. Down a short stairway is a semicircular wall that forms an excellent view over the former estuary of the river, an area now called Bramber Brooks, possibly because of the drainage works that crisscross it.

Moving along from the "Later Medieval Ruins" back to the gate tower we don't encounter anything of particular interest, except for being able to note how high the bailey lies over the estuary, and how steep the drop-off is! It should be clear that the castle is well-situated for defense, although in its long history as an active fortress it was never called upon to repel an attack.

VIEWS OF THE "LATER MEDIEVAL RUIN"

St. Nicholas Church

The only part of the castle that is still in use today for its original purpose is the church that was originally built over 950 years ago, which is dedicated to Saint Nicholas. It is one of the three church buildings of the Parish of Beeding and Bramber with Botolphs. The church of St. Peter in Upper Beeding is nearly as old as St. Nicholas, and was built on the orders of William de Braose, the same man who had St. Nicholas built. The St. Botolphs church, located a short distance to the south in the village of Botolphs, on the other hand, predates these other two, having been built originally by the Saxons.

PARISH CHURCH OF ST. NICHOLAS, BRAMBER, AD 1073

The St. Nicholas church seems very simple in its construction and decoration, but it has undergone many changes over its history. At some times in the past it had been described

The Parish Church of St.Nicholas Bramber Castle

This Parish Church was built by
William de Broase in 1073
as part of his
castle residences and defences.

Today it is the only part of
Bramber Castle still standing
and in regular use.

Visitors welcome

as "ruinous" and may not have been in active use during those times as a house of worship.

It was first built for a small college of secular canons[1], as well as for worship by the denizens of the castle. It wasn't long until it became clear that the church was inadequate for the accommodation of the canons, so de Braose had a more appropriately-sized facility built on the other side of the estuary in Saxon Sele, along with a church that was dedicated to Saints Peter and Andrew.

The St. Nicholas church was originally cruciform in plan. "Cruciform" means that its layout was in the form of a cross, the arms of the cross being called "transepts." The transepts were removed during later renovations, but evidence both inside and outside the church clearly shows their former presence.

The style and the decoration of the original structure suggests that de Braose had had Norman masons brought over to create the building. Some of the oldest masonry seems to be Caen limestone, which would have been brought over from Normandy, and was laid "ashlar," meaning that it was cut and shaped very precisely so that it required minimal amounts of mortar to bind it.

The low tower on the eastern end of the building was not originally part of the structure. It was built by the Reverend Dr. Thomas Green, who became the Rector of the parish in 1783 and worked tirelessly for the next 47 years restoring and then maintaining the building from the ruined state it was reported to have been in during a 1724 visit by the diocese's bishop. It is largely to Reverend Green's efforts that the modern church

---

[1] "Secular canons" are priests who live non-monastically.

survives in such a good state. Much work has been added to his over the decades, of course, but to him can be credited the church's survival.

Reverend Green remains associated with the church. Quite literally, in fact, since the remains of both he and his wife Ann, along with those of their eldest daughter (also named Ann) are interred in a vault within the church! This is commemorated in a plaque on the wall near the pulpit.

Among the other noteworthy decorations include the three-panel stained glass windows of the chancel behind the altar, probably from 1899, and the royal arms of Queen Anne (reigned 1707 – 1714), painted on wood and mounted on the south wall. Why Queen Anne? I've not been able to discover the reason why her arms in particular are displayed.

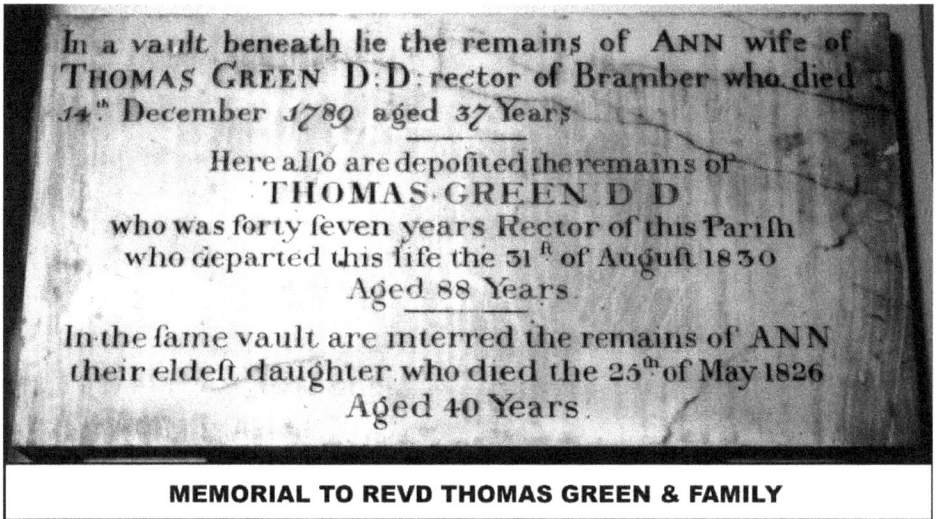

In a vault beneath lie the remains of ANN wife of THOMAS GREEN D:D rector of Bramber who died 14ᵗʰ December 1789 aged 37 Years

Here also are depofited the remains of
THOMAS GREEN D D
who was forty feven years Rector of this Parifh
who departed this life the 31ᴿ of Auguft 1830
Aged 88 Years

In the fame vault are interred the remains of ANN their eldeft daughter who died the 25ᵗʰ of May 1826
Aged 40 Years

MEMORIAL TO REVD THOMAS GREEN & FAMILY

Figure 16

22

Design and History

The castle is an example of the classic Norman *motte-and-bailey* design which was the pre-eminent style in medieval Europe at the time it was built. A motte-and-bailey castle has two basic parts: a fortified enclosure called a *bailey*, which has a curtain wall around its perimeter; and a *motte*, which is a mound – usually artificial – that is built next to or within the bailey and is surrounded by its own palisade and topped with a structure known as a *keep*. Motte and bailey castles are almost

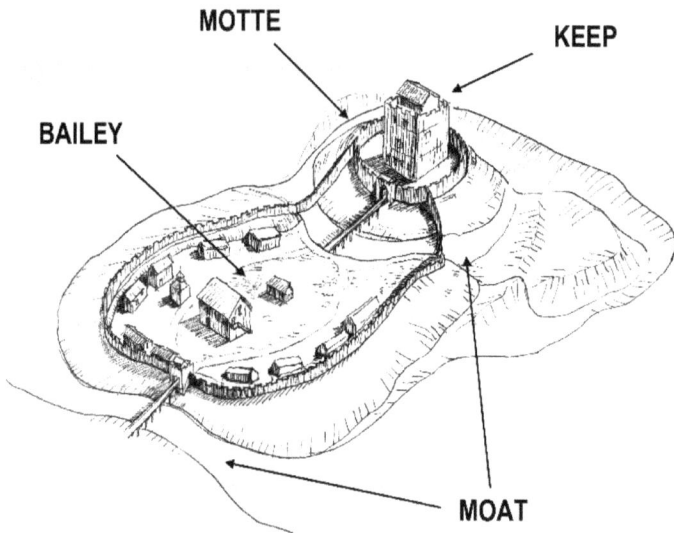

GENERAL PLAN OF A MOTTE-AND-BAILEY CASTLE

Figure 17

always surrounded by a deep ditch, or "moat."

23

The bailey normally contains the various service and residence buildings of the castle, and its palisade or curtain wall forms the castle's outer defense. The motte was the place of final defense, should an enemy penetrate the wall surrounding the bailey. The timber palisades of motte-and-bailey castles that were occupied for extended periods would generally be replaced by stone or masonry.

Though variations are frequent, the typical motte is sited on one side of the bailey, and features its own surrounding ditch and wall, as seen in the general plan of the basic motte-and-bailey castle above.

Bramber Castle's plan differs from the standard motte-and-bailey plan by having its motte placed more or less in the middle of its bailey (See figure 4 on page 6). This gave the bailey two parts, an outer part on the south end of the castle, with the inner bailey on its north. And as built originally, the motte's own defensive ditch began at the eastern side of the knoll, giving the western side of the motte the only level entrance to the inner bailey, and from thence, to the motte. The access ramp or stairs to the keep would have been located on the north side of the motte.

Other examples of the motte-and-bailey type which feature the same variation as Bramber Castle include two still-occupied castles, Windsor Castle, a residence of the monarch of the United Kingdom, and Arundel Castle, the residence of the Duke of Norfolk.

Motte-and-Bailey castles typically have a deep defensive ditch, called a moat, which surrounds both the bailey and the motte. The bailey's moat is normally integrated with the motte's moat. Moats are frequently thought of as being filled with water, but this isn't a requirement. Whether there is water in a given moat is a matter of what's available in the local area – if there's a river or lake next to the castle, it might be diverted into or channeled through the moat, but moats are frequently just dry ditches that are intended to make an assault across them very impractical.

Bramber Castle has a rather deep moat surrounding its bailey on its northern, western, and southern sides. There is a moat remnant on the eastern side, but since that side naturally plunges 22.8 meters (74.8 feet) down to the level of the tidal floodplain, or estuary, to the castle's east, an area called Bramber Brooks today, it is only nominally accurate to call it part of the moat. This is the only part of Bramber's moat which would have been regularly filled with water during its early history, due to the twice daily tides that filled the Adur's estuary and lapped up to the edge of the castle's knoll.

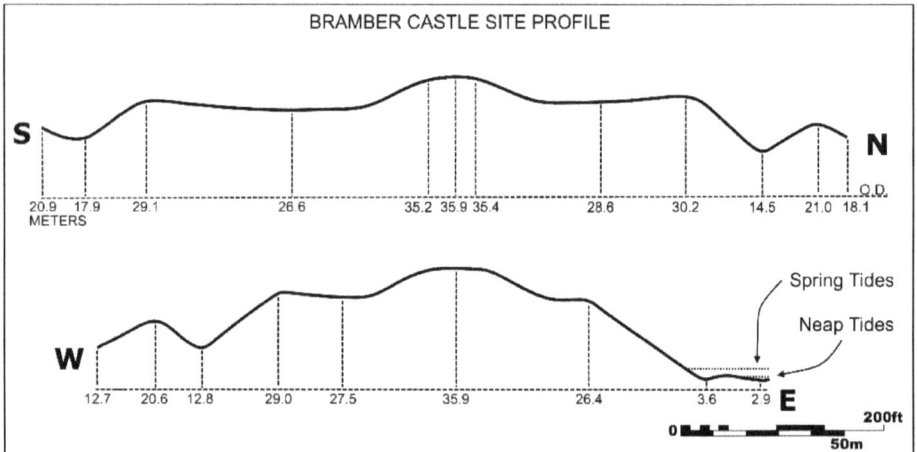

Figure 18

The approximate level of both highest spring and lowest neap high tides is shown on the eastern side of the castle's site profile above. Spring tides occur when both the moon and sun combine to make the largest high tides. Neap tides occur when the influence of the sun reduces the moon's influence on the height of the tide.

The full extent of the castle is not completely known. What remains of the castle's defensive works are only the most basic remnants. There were very likely some outer works guarding the approaches to the main gate and the bridge over the moat. As shown above, the stonework of just such a bridge still exists, although nothing remains of the bridge deck, and of course the space beneath what would have been the deck has been filled in. The stone structure that is visible has obvious holes in which wooden joists would have been inserted to support a wooden deck.

Since the church outside of the castle's curtain wall was part of the overall castle, it seems that it would have been within an outer ward or wall of the castle, if it had had any. Although no documentary evidence for outer wards exists, a rampart found to the southwest of the castle during the construction of the modern entrance from Castle Lane in 1926 may represent the western side of just such an outwork.

A speculative drawing of the castle, penned in 1938 by the artist J. G. Garratt shows a barbican[2] and an outer stone gateway surrounded by an outer southern wall. While no archaeological investigations have been made which might have uncovered remains of a barbican or outer gate, it's not outside the realm of possibility.

As suggested, Garratt's drawing is highly speculative, and should not be relied upon for historical accuracy. By

---

[2] A barbican (from Old French: *barbacane*) is a fortified outpost or fortified gateway, such as at an outer defense perimeter of a city or castle, or any tower situated over a gate or bridge which was used for defensive purposes.

coincidence, one aspect of the drawing is correct: the location of the main gate is shown to be on one side of the tower/keep at the entrance. This was the conclusion of the 1966/67 excavations, that while the roadway into the castle originally went through the tower's base, it was later shifted to the tower's side, when the tower's height was increased. Garratt entirely omits the "later medieval ruins" shown on the site map.

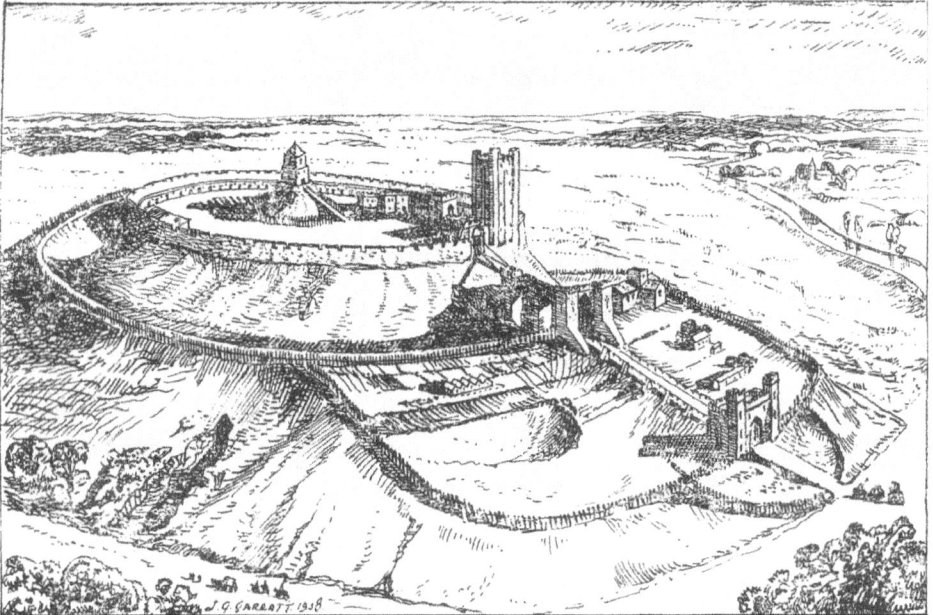

J. G. Garratt's Speculative Drawing

Figure 19

Whatever it looked like at its height, today's Bramber Castle is a husk of its former glory.

When the castle was first built there would have been a keep at the summit of the motte. And during the 1966/67 dig archaeologists found that there had been a moat or trench dug around the keep and within the outer bailey. This is shown in the diagram below.

27

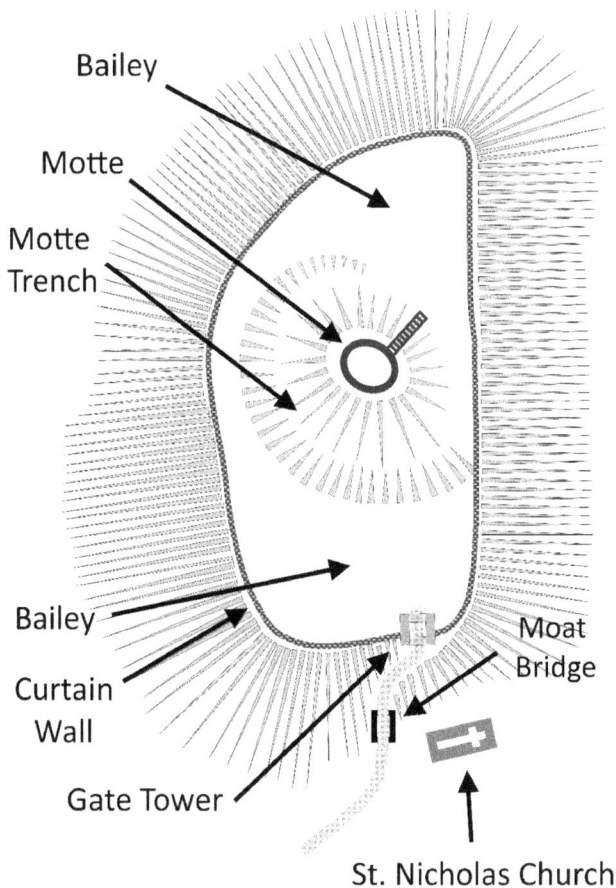

Bailey

Motte

Motte Trench

Bailey

Curtain Wall

Gate Tower

Moat

Bridge

St. Nicholas Church

Figure 20

The presence of squared and dressed flint knaps on the outside of some of the walls of the later medieval ruins (see below) suggested to the archaeologists that this structure may have been built in the 14th century, since such flint work was common in that period. Similar flints were also found in other places in the castle, and still others were found in some of the structures of Bramber village, evidently having been robbed away from the castle at some time after the castle stopped being maintained by its owners.

28

SQUARED AND DRESSED FLINT KNAPS

Figure 21

What remains of the stone curtain walls can be seen around much of the perimeter of the castle's knoll. Some of these stand up to 3 meters (10 feet) above the floor of the knoll. In places around the moat one can find some masonry fallen from the curtain wall. Researchers have decided that this was the result of ground instability due to excavation of the moat.

The most notable part of the castle is of course the one remaining wall of the gate tower. The fall of the other three walls would obviously have been a catastrophic event. When this occurred is unknown, but it was almost certainly sometime before the English Civil War (1642 to 1652), and it didn't happen all at once. This can be ascertained from the evidence of two sketches made by Wenceslas Hollar[3], a prolific and

---

[3] Also known as Václav Hollar, he was born in Prague in 1607 and died in London in 1677.

accomplished Bohemian graphic artist of the 17th century, who spent much of his life in England.

From 1636 to 1642 Hollar was employed in the household of Thomas Howard, the 21st Earl of Arundel, whose family owned Bramber Castle. Hollar entered his service when the Earl was on a diplomatic mission in Prague in 1635. But the Earl left England, never to return, at the start of the Civil War,

Bramber Castle from the South

Bramber Castle looking North from the Upper Bailey

Figure 22 - Wenceslas Hollar's drawings of the castle (pre-1640s)

which by implication would have marked the end of Hollar's employment with him. Hollar would have had no reason to visit Bramber after this. So, there seems to be good reason to assume that the sketches portray the condition of the castle well before the war.

Hollar's sketches show a gate tower with its southern wall absent, while the other three still stand. The cause of the gate tower's misfortune has been speculated in local legend as damage committed by Parliamentary forces during a supposed siege of the castle, but since the damage seems most likely to have occurred well before the Civil War, this legend is just that.

The legend does have a historical basis, however. It is documented that a skirmish between Parliamentary and Royalist forces did occur in the area. This skirmish involved the bridge over the Adur between the villages of Bramber and Upper Beeding. The legend claimed that a battery of artillery occupied the yard of St. Nicholas's church while firing at the castle. But since the battle involved custody of the bridge to the east, and the castle was by no means in condition to serve as an actual fortress[4], it can be surmised that the artillery was firing at the forces who held the bridge, especially since the church yard is raised ground with a good sight of the bridge. There's no documentary evidence for this, however[5].

The report of the archaeological dig that was done during 1966/67 tried to answer the question of when the moat was dug. This wasn't clear, and no archaeological evidence exists that points to a particular time period. Documents in connection with the management of the castle specify that the moat was widened and perhaps deepened during the reign of King John, sometime between 1208 and 1216, during a time when the de

---

[4] Whereas the castle belonged to the family of the Earl of Arundel, they did not live there. By the 1550s, it was recorded as 'the late castle', used was for grazing.

[5] Descriptions of the brief battle made by a Parliamentary commander say nothing about the use of the churchyard in the engagement.

Braose family was outlawed and the King had possession. This is discussed later in this narrative.

For reasons I will go into a bit later, I feel that the moat was originally dug within the first few years after the castle's construction. That there were improvements made to it later, that's not a reason to believe that the moat didn't exist beforehand. For one thing, there would have been concerns over the defensibility of the castle which only a moat would have solved.

And ground instability need not have caused the fall of all three of the lost walls. Once the south wall had fallen, the remaining three would have been structurally weakened enough that storms and normal weathering (not to mention deliberate material removal by local residents) could have gradually led to the fall of the others.

Why is the Castle Here?

Looking at a map of Sussex, we see that Bramber castle is near the coast, just 9 miles northwest of Brighton and 5 miles north-northeast of Worthing. It's situated on a knoll above the River Adur, one of the major historic commercial rivers of Sussex.

The castle would have been built in this location for two reasons:

1. To help defend the natural invasion route from the coast through the valley of the River Adur, a route which the Danes and Vikings had used previously to raid inland; and

2. To protect and control the town of Steyning, which despite its obvious inland location, was an important port during medieval times.

The castle was built on a knoll overlooking both Steyning and the river and tidal flats leading up to it. It was a natural place of defense, and though it was thought by some that the location may have been used by the Saxons as a place of fortification, there is no written or significant archaeological evidence of this. The site of the village that grew up around the castle, which came to be called Bramber as well, also has no evidence of Saxon occupation, and lying on a portion of the estuary, it was normally under water at high tide.

The natural knoll on which Bramber Castle stands rises about 120 feet above the level of the river Adur and is somewhat D-shaped. North to south it is now 560 feet long and 280 feet wide, east to west. The site is relatively level. It isn't known whether the top of the knoll was sculpted by the

Normans for the castle, or if that was how it was naturally formed.

The knoll sticks out somewhat from the chalk formation of the South Downs and forms a kind of peninsula into the River Adur's old estuary. It appears to be the kind of feature called by geologists a "meander core." Such features form as rivers wander or meander in response to bank erosion. Dramatic meanders can be seen in the wandering of more mighty rivers, such as the Colorado in the USA, which have carved out amazing "meander cores" over their history. In the case of the Adur, as the last glaciation came to an end twelve thousand years ago, melt water from the glaciers would have been responsible for the Adur's cutting through the chalk of the South Downs, and the formation of the knoll on which Bramber Castle was built in 1071.

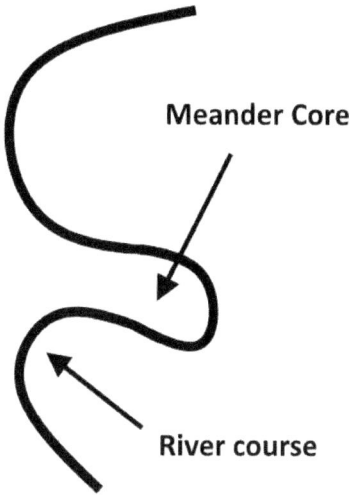

Figure 23 - Meander Core

When the castle was built, the Adur estuary flooded twice daily with the tides. But it was fully open to the English Channel in the more distant past, and was probably more of a shallow bay than an estuary during Roman times.

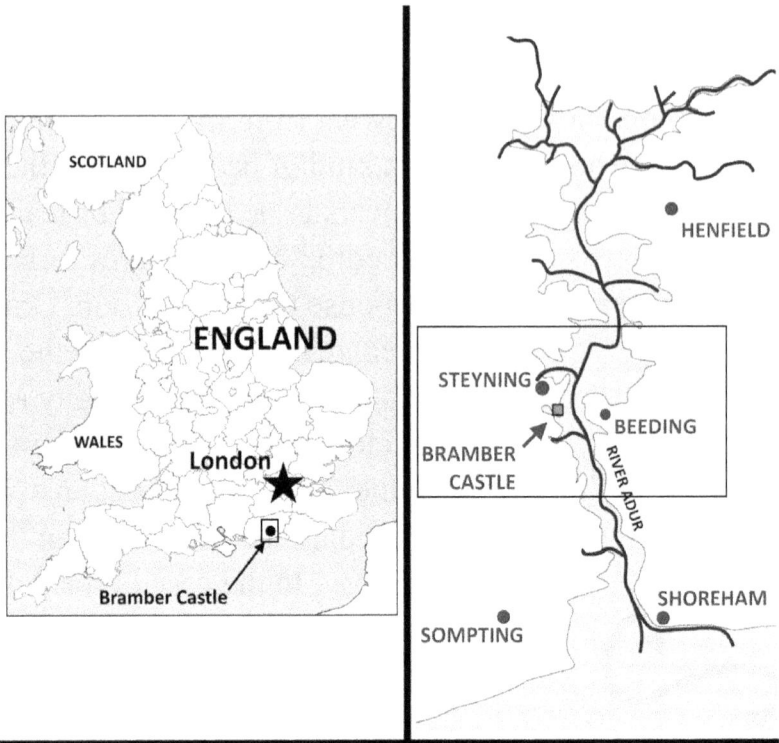

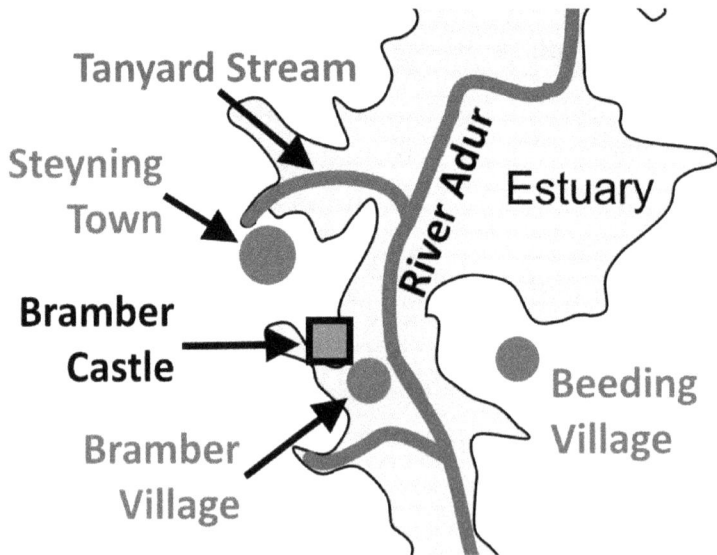

SCOTLAND

ENGLAND

WALES

London

Bramber Castle

HENFIELD

STEYNING

BEEDING

BRAMBER
CASTLE

RIVER ADUR

SOMPTING

SHOREHAM

Tanyard Stream

Steyning
Town

River Adur

Estuary

Bramber
Castle

Beeding
Village

Bramber
Village

Figure 24

Historical Background

To understand Bramber Castle in the context of England, it would be helpful to know something about the historical backdrop that led to the castle's construction.

The history of England as a kingdom began in 927, when the Anglo-Saxon ruler Æthelstan managed to take control of most of what we know today as England, which consisted of the island of Great Britain from the Scottish border in the north to the English Channel in the south, except for Wales. This made Æthelstan the first English king. Of course, before Æthelstan there had been kings who had ruled over substantial parts of this area, such as Alfred the Great, but Æthelstan was the first true King of England.

This kingdom of England continued for the next 139 years. Since Æthelstan never married and had no children, England was not ruled by his descendants, but by descendants of his father, Edward the Elder. This was not without interruption: there was a 26-year period when England was ruled over by Danes, from 1016 to 1042, starting with the legendary Cnut the Great[6].

The last descendant of Æthelstan's family to be King of England was Edward the Confessor. Unfortunately, in January 1066 he died without heirs, and there arose a dispute over who

---

[6] This is the famous King Cnut who is supposed to have commanded the incoming tide not to wet his feet – the story is sometimes told to show how full of himself he was. Shouldn't the tide obey the King? However, the full story is that Cnut was teaching that his power was limited. It is supposed that after the tide ignored his command, he said "Let all the world know that the power of kings is empty and worthless, and there is no king worthy of the name save Him by whose will heaven, earth and the sea obey eternal laws."

should then sit on the throne of England. The Duke of Normandy, William, had apparently been promised the throne by Edward some time before his death, confirmation of which had allegedly been given to him by Edward's brother-in-law, Harold Godwinson, during an official visit. But on his deathbed, Edward allegedly changed his mind and named his brother-in-law to be his successor[7]. Harold was subsequently confirmed as king by the Witenagemot, or "council of advisors" to the King.

Duke William took great offense at this seeming betrayal and began planning for an invasion of England. According to William of Poitiers, considered by many scholars to be a reasonably reliable source, shortly before the Battle of Hastings William received an envoy from Harold who admitted that Edward had indeed promised the throne to William, but argued that his deathbed promise to Harold overrode Edward's previous promise. In his response, William did not dispute the deathbed promise but contended that Edward's prior promise to him took precedence.

In any event, resolution of the matter came down to war.

The Leadup to Duke William's Invasion

The invasion did not take place immediately; it was delayed both by William's preparations and then by contrary weather. Harold was quite ready for William's arrival, and he had raised a substantial force to meet it. Unfortunately, William's delay dragged into harvest time, and Harold was

---

[7] These "promises" were one of the mechanisms that Edward used to keep potential enemies happy, by hinting they might succeed him. Likely as not Edward intended Harold to be his true successor, but unfortunately didn't make this clear.

forced to release the *fyrd*, or the part of his army who could only be held to service in the army temporarily[8]. These were needed at home to help harvest fall crops.

To add to Harold's woes, Tostig, one of Harold's brothers, had earlier been outlawed and removed as Earl of Northumberland by King Edward. Tostig wanted to be restored to his lands and power, and had been working from his place of exile in France to ally himself with another claimant to the English throne, the Norwegian king Harald Sigurdsson, called Hardrada[9]. Tostig and Hardrada came to an agreement to join forces to throw Harold off his new throne. They may also have been working in loose concert with William to help destabilize the situation in England at the time of William's invasion. Subsequent events seem to suggest this may have been the case.

Accordingly, Tostig and Hardrada and their substantial allied army arrived in northern England, taking York after prevailing at the Battle of Fulford on 20 September 1066.

King Harold had rushed northwards to meet this threat, and five days after Fulford he surprised and defeated Hardrada and Tostig at the Battle of Stamford Bridge. Both Hardrada and Tostig perished in the fight, and their army suffered significant casualties.

While Harold had been dealing with the invasion in the north, William's own invasion force had finally departed Normandy for England. They arrived in Sussex, near Pevensey, just three days after Harold's victory at Stamford Bridge. They were not met by much armed resistance, since King Harold's

---

[8] At this time the fyrd consisted of a nucleus of experienced soldiers that would be supplemented by ordinary villagers and farmers from the shires who would accompany their lords.

[9] In the old sagas this was written as *harðráði*. In modern Norwegian it is Hardråde – and is roughly translated as "stern counsel" or "hard ruler."

forces were in the far north of England repelling the invasion there. William's forces first captured Pevensey Castle, an old former Roman fortification that at the time held only a token garrison, and then the town and port of Hastings.

Harold and his army would still have been tired from their march northwards and the battle, but Harold knew that he dare not linger in the north. Accordingly, he got his army back on its feet and they force-marched the 240 miles back southwards. Sometime along the way, he would have received news of William's landing in Sussex.

And so it was on 12 October 1066 that Harold's exhausted forces met William's at a location just seven miles north of Hastings. The sizes of their forces were similar, but the English were defending on a low hill, and thus they held somewhat of an advantage. However, the English force consisted entirely of infantry, whereas William fielded infantry, archers, and cavalry. The combined arms on the Norman side gave William an advantage that probably neutralized Harold's defensive posture. The battle raged all day, but at the end a Norman tactic caused Harold's right flank to become disorganized. This disorganization was then exploited by the Normans, and the English forces were put to flight. It was during this phase that King Harold was killed, reputedly by an arrow in his eye.

William's position as the now de facto ruler of England was formalized 11 weeks later, on Christmas Day, when he was crowned as the King of England. It was this conquest which caused him to ever afterwards be known as William the Conqueror.

King William's Consolidation of Power

When William first took control of England, his position as king was not at all completely secure. Although the Anglo-Saxon nobility had acquiesced to his rule, they were nevertheless not all that keen on it, and Norse raiders were still a possible problem. Therefore, to keep William's new kingdom firmly under control, he needed to have a secure base in England. Because the ancient county of Sussex was directly across from William's homeland in Normandy, that secure base had to be Sussex.

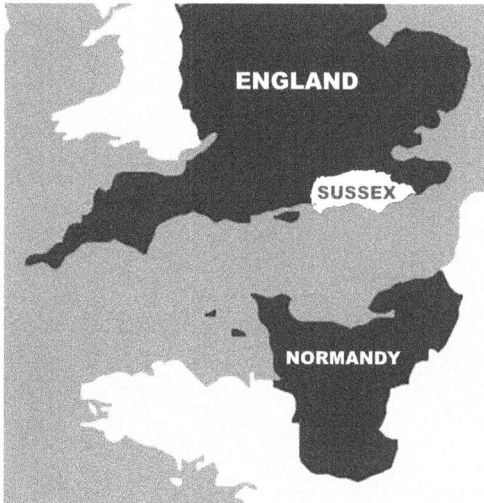

Under the Anglo-Saxons, the governance of Sussex consisted of a set of four administrative areas, called "rāps" in Old English, or "rapes" in modern English[10]. From west to east,

---

[10] In Old English the word was rāp (rope) pronounced approximately "rahp" and its meaning was related to the idea of a rope forming a boundary line. Similar to Old English, the Dutch cognate word *reep* means a jurisdictional area, and likewise descends from the West Germanic word for "rope". The modern term "rape," meaning sexual violence, derives from an entirely different word in old French, "raper," meaning to seize

their names were Arundel, Lewes, Pevensey, and Hastings, which were the names of their principal towns. King William gave the administration of each rape into the hands of one of the loyal retainers who had accompanied him during the invasion and who had fought on his side in the Battle of Hastings.

The "Rapes" or administrative areas of Sussex

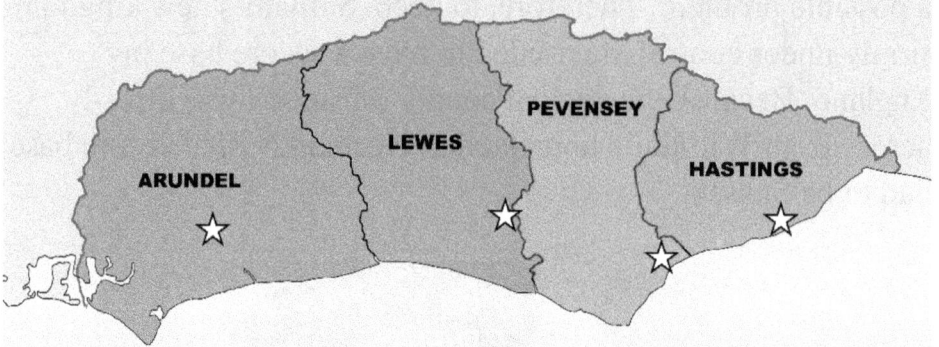

1067 AD

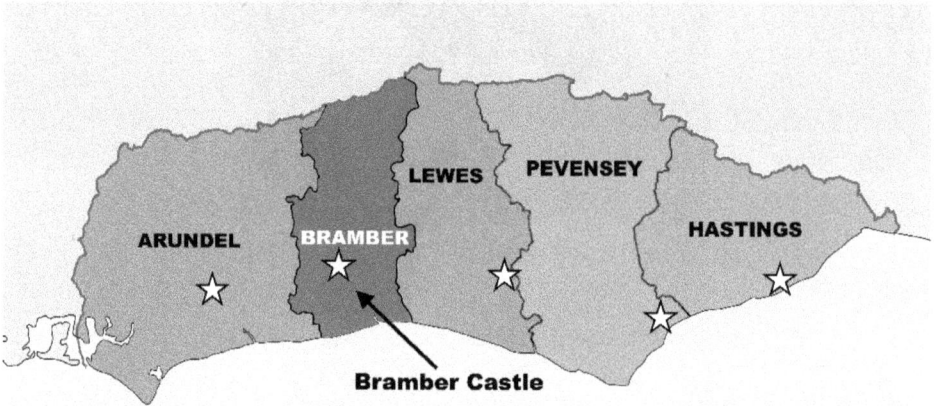

Bramber Castle

☆ = "Caput" or seat of administration

1073 AD

These four districts remained unchanged for only about five years. It was then that William created a new one between Arundel and Lewes, using land from each. The new rape was centered on the River Adur, whose large estuary led up to

---

or take by force.

Steyning, the important port town. One might think that the name of the new rape should have been named Steyning after its principal town, as was the case with the other rapes. But this isn't what happened.

The river that the rape was centered on was not called the Adur in 1073. This was the name given to the river sometime in the early 1600s, based on the mistaken idea that the town of Shoreham, the coastal town at the river's mouth, was the site of the ancient Roman fort called *Portus Adurni*. This was incorrect, and the true site was later discovered to be 38 miles to the west, at the north end of Portsmouth Harbour in Hampshire, and was nowhere near this river. But the name Adur stuck.

Another name for the river that was used for a time was the Sore. This appeared in an old book that was published in 1577, *Description of England*. The apparent cause of the river being called Sore, was due to its flowing through Shoreham into the English Channel, which was often spelled "Soreham" in early sources. It isn't hard to see why this correspondence was arrived at, since rivers and the towns associated with each other do occasionally share their names or parts of names with each other.

But the Rape of Bramber was called by that name because that was the name of the River Adur at the time of the Norman conquest in 1066: the River Bramber.

The name Bramber is considered by some authorities likely to relate to the area and predates the castle and settlement. In this case the name is claimed to derive from Old English *brēmer*, meaning 'broom-thicket', or from 'bramble-thicket', and had been adopted for the river by 956.

Other authorities reject the idea that Adur is a relatively new coining for the river's name. The Adur-Worthing Council website claims that the name Adur is from an old Celtic word, "Dwyr," meaning "water."[11] If true, "Bramber" would be a later name for the river. And this wouldn't be unusual. Many place names in England do go back to Celtic times.

The Importance of Steyning

Even though the name of the Rape was not Steyning, Steyning was nevertheless its most important town. Its importance grew from the large amount of commerce which passed through it, and this was because at that time the River Adur and its estuary were fully navigable up to the town. Steyning is about 6 miles inland from the Channel, and the ocean-going ships of the time could easily sail or row all the way up to Steyning to offload and take on cargoes, and the estuary itself was a safe harbor from storms.

It is difficult to establish how many people resided at Steyning at the time of the Conquest, but Steyning's position on the boundary between the downland and the Sussex Weald, and its nearness to navigable water was what made it a centre of trade; moreover, Steyning's church was a royal minster church dedicated to the Anglo-Saxon Saint Cuthman. His remains were buried in the church, and these relics are said to have attracted pilgrims, and the money the pilgrims spent in the town benefited the local economy as well.

The town of Steyning was important not only to the economy of this area of Sussex, but St. Cuthman's church was

---

[11] There seems to be some basis for this. Welsh is a Celtic language, and the word for "water" in Welsh is "dŵr,"

also an important source of income for whomever happened to be the beneficiary of the large manor estate that was associated with it. It is here that the monks of the Benedictine abbey of Fécamp, in Normandy, become important. Because Anglo-Saxon King Edward the Confessor had been sheltered and protected by the Normans during a period of exile, in 1047 he had granted the royal minster church in Steyning to the abbey. With its large, wealthy manor lands and thriving port, this grant was a great asset for the abbey.

But the monks didn't have long to profit from this grant when just five years later, in 1052, Godwin, the Earl of Wessex, expelled them from Steyning and seized the church estate for himself[12]. When upon his death in 1053 his son Harold ascended to the Earldom, Harold chose to keep it, rather than restore it to the abbey. There were very good economic and strategic reasons for this. The Steyning church estate was a lucrative property and provided substantial income; and as Harold probably already had his eye on the kingship of England, if he were to leave Fécamp Abbey in charge at Steyning, it would have represented a Norman toehold at a potential invasion port.

As it turned out, this affront to Fécamp Abbey was one of the causes that William the Conqueror put forward as a justification for his 1066 bid to conquer England. Upon setting out upon the invasion, William did receive material support from Fécamp after he swore to restore Steyning to the Abbey – which oath he fulfilled after defeating Harold at Hastings.

---

[12] Why wouldn't King Edward have objected to this? Maybe he did, but the Earl's power rivaled that of the king, even though he was nominally subordinate to him, and this doubtless would have contributed to the king's failure to do anything about it.

As Harold had known, and as William the Conqueror had likewise recognized, the easy navigability of the Adur River estuary made it easy for enemies to invade deep into Sussex. A stronghold was needed to make such potential invaders think twice about it, and this was the likely reason why King William created the new Rape of Bramber. And this would have been why the administration of the rape was given to one of the Conqueror's trusted Norman lords.

The Lords of Bramber

In the book's chapter headings whose subjects are the Lords of Bramber I wanted to include their birth and death years to indicate both the man's lifetime as well as his period of tenureship as lord. However, vital statistics records for the period of time this book covers are quite spotty. In many cases not even years of birth for the people who are described are just not found. But external events can help estimate them with some degree of reasonability. In these headings, if I haven't been able to find or cannot reasonably estimate a birth year, I will indicate this with question marks. If I give an estimated year that I am not reasonably confident of, I'll indicate this with a question mark after the year.

The "Many Williams" Problem

Now just a note on terminology to help us avoid confusion as I tell about the de Braose family.

The point of confusion I'm worried about is the "Many Williams" problem. The name William was very popular in the de Braose family, and that name was also shared by the first two kings of England during this time. In the de Braose family, most of the Lords of Bramber were named William. So, when I say "William de Braose" the problem is, which William? I could solve this by saying "William the First," but then we run into the fact that William the Conqueror, who as king was closely connected to the de Braoses, was also "William the First."

I'm going to solve this by using the cardinal form of the number for de Braoses instead of the ordinal, which I will reserve for the kings of England. Cardinal, by the way, means the number itself, for example, "One". The ordinal form of the number one, on the other hand, is "First", because it refers to the *order* in which it comes.

So, using the Roman numeral, William I ("the First") or William II ("the Second") refers to a *King* William. But using the Arabic numeral, William 1 ("One") or William 2 ("Two") refers to a *Lord* William. And if I include the surname or lordship name, such as "de Braose", I will write, for example, William 2 de Braose.

In the pages that follow you will find two Williams who were never Lords of Bramber, but who could have been if circumstances had been otherwise. I number these two along with the others, and they are William 4, the son of William 3, and William 5, the son of Reginald. Because they were never Lords of Bramber, they receive no chapters of their own, but are discussed in their fathers' chapters.

Braose: a House and a Surname

This House was a prominent family of Anglo-Norman nobles originating in Briouze, near Argentan, Orne, Normandy.
In Latinized form, the name has also been recorded as "de Braiosa". The surname has descended to modern times as "Breuse," "Brewes," "Brehuse," "Briouze," "Brewose," etc. "Brewer" may also be a form of the surname, but this is also an occupational surname, like "Cooper" or "Carpenter," so it's not a reliable indicator.

THE HOUSE OF BRAOSE

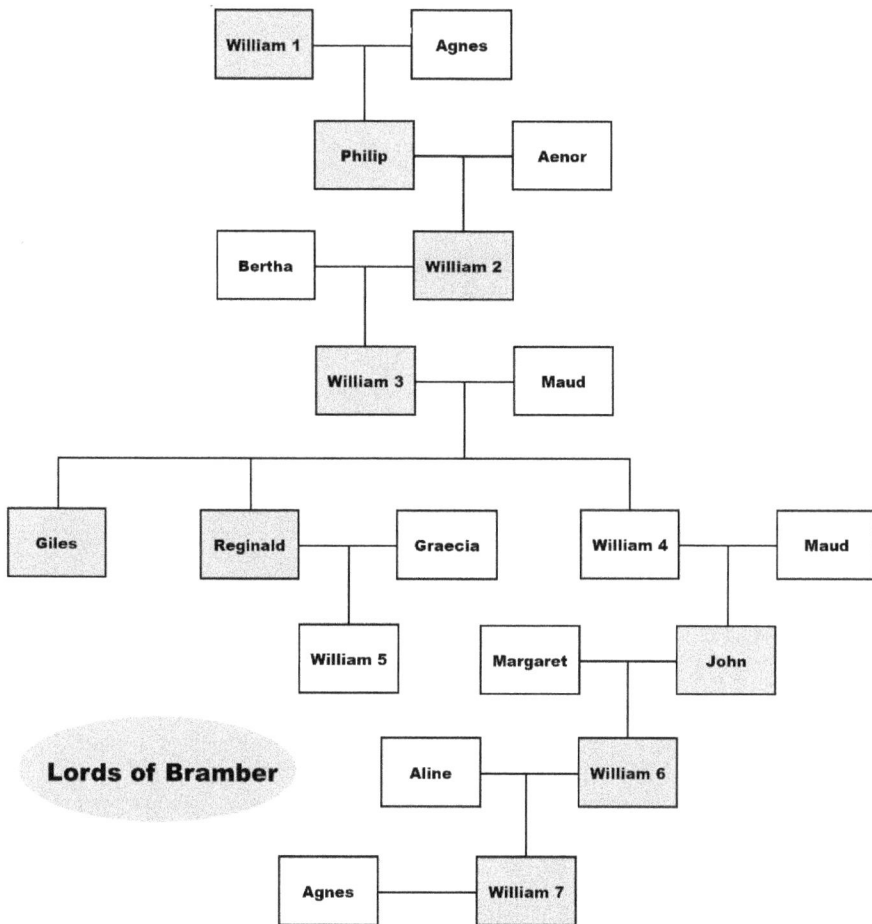

Lords of Bramber

48

William 1 de Braose

1st Lord of Bramber

Life: ??? – 1094
Tenure: 1071 – 1094

One of the lords who was allied with Duke William in his conquest of England was a man named *Guillaume de Briouze* in his native tongue, which was Norman French. *Guillaume* of course is the French equivalent of William in Modern English. And he was *de Briouze,* meaning "of Briouze," because he was the Lord of Briouze, a region and town in Normandy. However, the name comes down to us in English as *de Braose*, making him known as William de Braose.

He may or may not have been at the Battle of Hastings (the extant records do not mention him as one of those who fought there), but he was certainly a loyal supporter of the Conqueror.

His appointment as the Lord of Bramber in 1071 certainly reflected high trust and regard in King William's eyes. De Braose and his descendants held that lordship over Bramber, with one brief interruption, for the next 250 years.

According to some sources, William 1 de Braose was born around 1049, probably in Briouze, Normandy. He was not only Lord of Briouze and Bramber, but the Conqueror gave him other lands in Sussex, as well as land in Dorset in the area around Wareham and Corfe, two manors in Surrey, as well as one each in Berkshire at Southcote, and at Downton in Wiltshire[13].

Besides administering the Rāp of Bramber, William continued to support the Conqueror by fighting alongside him in campaigns in England, as well as in Normandy and Maine in France. A pious man, Lord William also granted land and funds for the building of a number of religious institutions in both France and England.

William was married to Agnes de St. Clare and later possibly to Eve de Boissey (who was the widow of Anchetil de Harcourt). It is not known which of these wives was the mother of his son and heir, Philip, but since Philip seems to have been born when William was in his twenties, it was probably Agnes. Did he have other children we know nothing about? It seems likely, given the usages of the age. The de Braose name occurs in other family lines, and in various forms, so we can conclude that there may be many others for whom no firm connection with the main de Braose line can be established due to the lack of surviving records.

First Stage Construction of the Castle

As mentioned earlier, Bramber castle was initially built as a motte-and-baily of the central motte style. As with many such castles, the motte featured its very own moat. In this case, the moat was dug on the south side of the motte, so as to block the eastern side of the moat, making the inner bailey's entrance on the west. The bottom of the north side of the motte was even

---

[13] Upon mention of Downton, perhaps you might think to yourself that William had something to with Downton Abbey? Ah, wouldn't that be nice! But the fictional television program Downton Abbey is set in Yorkshire, a couple hundred miles north of de Braose's Downton in Wiltshire. And you might be further interested to know that while there are six towns or villages named Downton in the British Isles, there is no actual Downton Abbey.

with the floor of the bailey, and it can be assumed that there was a stairway leading to the top of the motte. No excavation has been done of the motte itself, nevertheless it must be the case that there was a final defensive keep on the top. Whether it was constructed of timber or stone is unknown.

The earth needed to build the motte would have been dug up initially from its defensive moat, but the dimensions of the motte suggest that more material would have had to have been brought in from outside the castle walls. And given that a surrounding moat would have been in the plans anyway, additional material would have been dug from there. This would have begun from the place where the bridge remains are now found, in order to increase the castle's defensibility.

It must be kept in mind that this was merely five years after the Conquest, England was still not entirely pacified, and would not be so for many years to come. So defensive fortifications would continue to be very necessary.

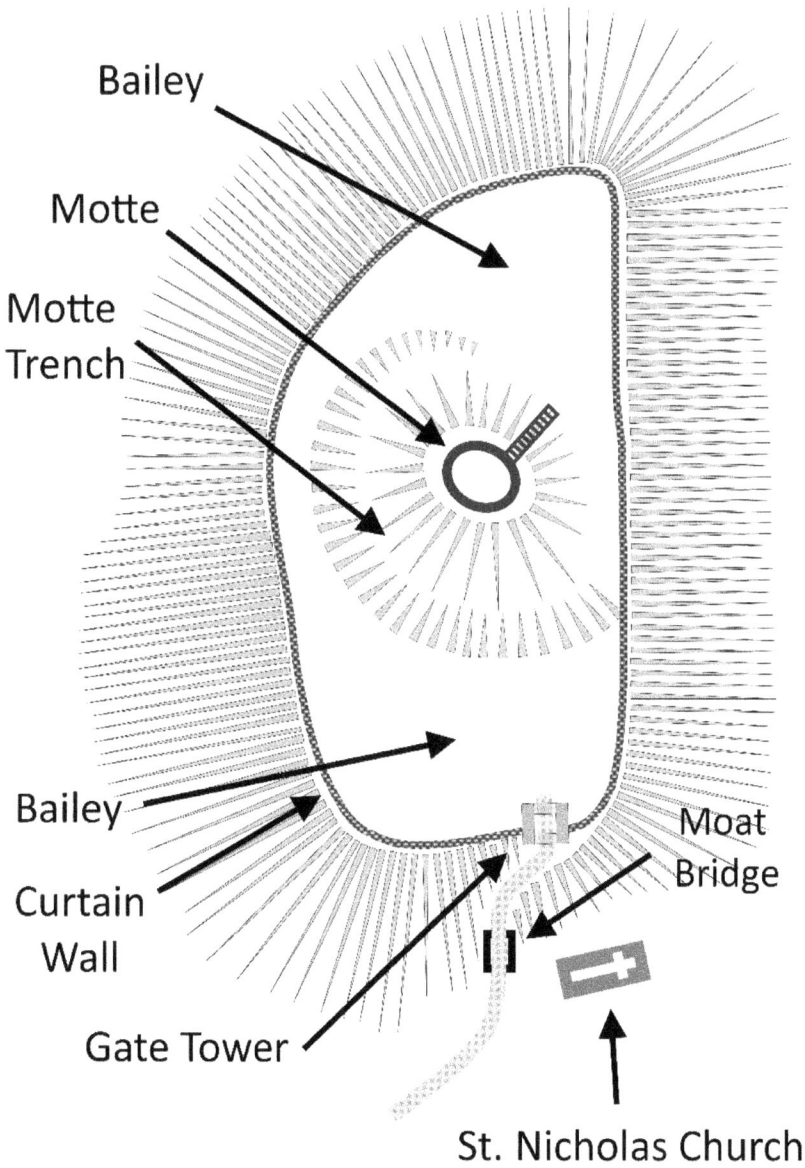

Bailey

Motte

Motte
Trench

Bailey

Curtain
Wall

Gate Tower

Moat
Bridge

St. Nicholas Church

Figure 25 - Initial construction of Bramber Castle, to include a motte moat

The Castle's Conversion to the Enclosure Type

It isn't known at what time it happened, but not long after the completion of the motte-and-bailey version of the castle, de Braose had it converted to a different style, a style which eliminated the motte's own defensive ditch by filling it in, partly from material on the motte. The keep may have been dismantled as well.

It isn't known when the wooden palisade walls were replaced with stone. The period of the outer moat's creation is likewise unknown, although it shouldn't have been long before at least part of it was dug. The archaeological investigations in 1966/67 decided that it had been dug sometime during the 1200s AD by King John after he confiscated the de Braose properties. This author respectfully begs to differ with that opinion, however. He believes that there is insufficient support for the idea.

There is documentary evidence that King John had the moat deepened or extended after wresting custody of the castle from the de Braoses. But there is sufficient reason to believe that the moat was built during the administration of the first William de Braose. The reasons for this are set out below.

The Causeway, Bridges, and Bramber Village

The current village of Bramber at the castle's foot did not exist at the time of the Norman conquest. Its site, which is low ground between the castle and the Saxon village of Beeding, would have been under water at high tide, and would have been a mud flat at low tide. Permanent structures could not have been built where the village exists today.

Castles normally have villages associated with them, and form naturally due to the need for services[14] that are not easily conducted in the castles themselves. At Bramber castle there was sufficient dry land for a settlement on the west side of the castle, so one might expect the village to have grown up there. But it grew out on the tidal mud flats instead! This seems mysterious, but it would have come about because de Braose decided to link the castle with Beeding village, by building a road on a causeway across the mud flats and two bridges over the River Adur. Two bridges were necessary because at the time there were two main river channels to cross, one of them being much wider than the other. The narrower channel was the one closer to Beeding village, but today it is the only channel.

A couple of questions present themselves in connection with the expense of building this crossing. The first question is why? And the second question is how? The answers to these questions aren't hard to figure out.

At the time the castle was built there seems to have been no convenient way of crossing the River Adur in its southern reaches. Old documents mention that there was a ferry operating at a narrows on the river near St. Botolphs church even before the Norman conquest, but ferries are intermittent. No bridges over the Adur are mentioned.

The advantages of a permanent crossing such as a bridge include the ability to cross a river regardless of the time of day (and the vagaries of tides). And a bridge offers the opportunity for charging tolls for crossing it. Since a bridge at this point on the Adur would draw a lot of traffic, income from the tolls would be substantial.

---

[14] Such as the proverbial "butcher, baker, and candlestick maker."

As to how, consider the problem: the Adur is quite tidal, and twice a day the tide would have filled and then drained the river's estuary with salty water. In order to place a permanent structure on such an estuary, one must pile up material so as to keep it above the level of the high tide.

Land is valuable, for there is only so much of it. People living next to shallow seas that go through cycles of shallow water and then mud often come up with the idea that if they could exclude the water in certain places, they could dry up the mud and use the new dry land for more valuable purposes. In the English language, there are words for the process of creating new land from oceans, seas, riverbeds or lake beds. In modern days, this is called *land reclamation*. In the olden days of Britain, this process was called *inning*[15], a now obsolete term, with the verb form probably being "to inn."

Typically, this is done even today by first building some kind of cofferdam out into a section of water, such that the cofferdam is able to exclude water from entering, or at least slow it down from doing so. And then the area from which water has been excluded is gradually filled in with rocks and dirt, forming dry ground. The most famous example of this kind of land reclamation is perhaps the polders of The Netherlands, with its marvelous system of dikes and pumping stations. Without such a system it is estimated that up to 65% of that country would be under water at high tide.

Alternatively, without a cofferdam rock and dirt could simply be piled onto mud flats high enough to stand above the tide.

---

[15] Besides referring to a period within certain games, such as cricket or baseball, "inning" also has the meanings "the act of reclaiming marshy or flooded land," or "an enclosure, as of wasteland."

England has its own examples of extensive inning. Not so famous as that of The Netherlands are the former tidelands of London, which were part of the Thames River estuary. The inning of the Thames was begun in Roman times, and without that land reclamation (and the tidal dam), today's Houses of Parliament, along with a large number of other historical structures, would be flooded at high tide. Additionally, we have the Fens in East Anglia and the Dungeness Peninsula in East Sussex and Kent, both of which were in ancient times tidal basins and salt marshes, but which today are rich agricultural lands that still lie only slightly above sea level.

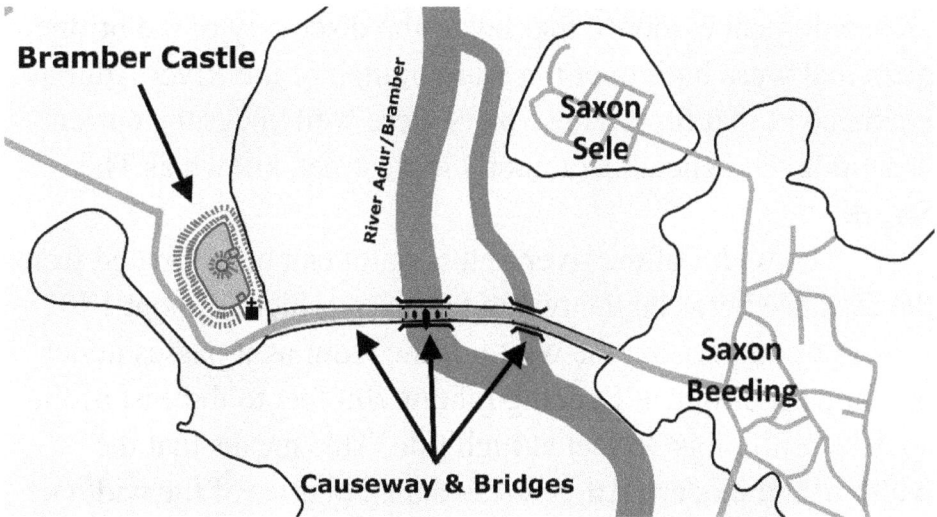

Finally, we come back to Bramber village and the bridge over the River Adur. It is about 2,000 feet from the castle to Beeding village. That's a lot of mud flat to turn into dry ground! So where does one get material for the purpose? The answer to that question would no doubt have occurred to de Braose as the answer to another question that would have arisen at the time he dug out the moat around the castle. This question would have been, "What do we do with all this dirt?"[16]

The moat on three sides of the castle is up to 80 feet deep, forming a V-shaped ditch that is up to 100 feet across at the top, about 10 feet across at the bottom, and totaling about 1,500 feet in length. Without getting into the mathematics of the volume of a trapezoidal solid (which this approximates), this represents material of about 6,600,000 cubic feet in volume. This is probably an upper limit, since the moat is 80 feet deep only at its deepest point, on the west side. And then one must consider that not all of it was dug out at that time.

The larger of the two bridges that de Braose had built no longer exists, but its location was discovered in 1974, during construction of a drain line in Bramber. The builders found archaeological evidence that led to the discovery of the bridge piers that were built over the main branch of the River Adur as it existed at that time. These piers were well under the current ground level, beneath Bramber's high street, known as The Street.

The width of the river at this point can be estimated from the distance between the two outer piers, which is about 170 feet. For comparison, the width of the Adur as it passes under the modern bridge at Beeding (about 700 feet to the east of the ancient bridge), is 38 feet at high tide. This means that the width of the modern Adur is less than a quarter of the width of the ancient Adur.

---

[16] It wouldn't have been all dirt, however. The knoll of the castle is a "meader core" consisting of what is called "lower chalk", and so the bulk of the material dug from the moat would have been chalky material.

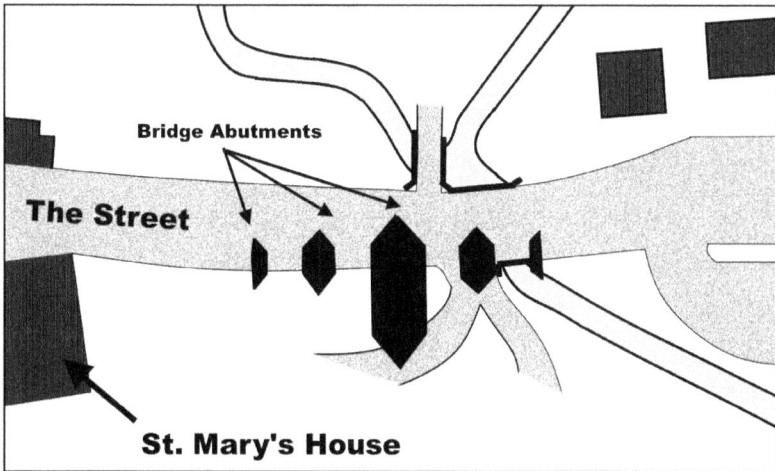

Buried well below ground level are the five bridge abutments of the bridge over what was the main stream of the River Adur. Only a small unobtrusive drain stream remains.

Figure 26

In order to arrive at the westernmost pier of that bridge from the likely location of the eastern side of the castle's outer works (down the hill about a hundred feet from the churchyard), a distance of about 2,000 feet, one would have to cross about 800 feet of mud flat at low tide. In modern times, the highest spring tide comes in at about 21.7 feet or 6.6 meters above the "ordnance datum," or mean sea level. Additionally on the other side of the bridge, it is about 600 feet further until one reaches what was a second bridge over a narrower branch of the Adur (now the sole course of the river). On the other side of that branch, there would have been a little more mud flat to cross, perhaps 360 feet further, until one reached dry ground.

If we assume that sea levels and tides have not much changed since the 11th century (perhaps a dangerous assumption to make), this means that in order to cross between these bridges over those mud flats on more-or-less dry ground at high

58

tide, it would be necessary to dump material along a path totaling 1,760 feet in length, to a height of at least 22 feet above mean sea level. If we had dug 6.6 million cubic feet of material out of the ground comprising the castle's moat, this would enable us to build a causeway using that material which might be 170 feet wide – enough for a road crossing the estuary that allowed some structures, such as houses or inns, to be built on either side.

De Braose's old bridge abutments lie beneath this bridge and culvert

Figure 27 - De Braose's bridge is under this one

As seen in Figure 25, the larger bridge was 170 feet long with five piers, and its central pier was large enough that it had space for a small chapel, dedicated to Saint Mary. Of course, the bridge no longer exists[17]. Changes in the river's course over

---

[17] Actually, it does still exist, after a fashion, but it's just a flat span passing over a culvert. That once mighty stream of the Adur has been reduced to what amounts to a flood-control drain. The bridge over it is unnoticeable as a bridge, unless one pays attention while walking past it. See Figure 26.

the centuries made the bridge unnecessary, and its material was gradually robbed away for other purposes.

A facility nearby, called Saint Mary's House, was built in 1470 as a monastic hostel for pilgrims and a home for the monks who collected the tolls at the bridge. It still remains, and the building is now open seasonally as a tea-house, with beautiful gardens featuring topiary figures, and a quite large secret garden at the back. The house has a music room featuring two 14th-century ornately carved stone chantry tombs serving as fireplaces, and is regularly used for concerts and recitals.

Another reason to support the idea of a moat during William 1's time was one of the causes of the dispute he had with the Fécamp abbey. Not far from his bridge, de Braose caused two facilities built that the abbey objected to. The one was a quay from where he imposed passage or landing fees on cargoes heading further up the river towards Steyning. This was in direct competition to the landing fees that the abbey charged at the quays in Steyning. And by undercharging, this would have negatively impacted the abbey's income, since the new

roadway at Bramber village made it possible to avoid Steyning altogether!

The second part of the problem was a branch channel that de Braose had dug from the river to the foot of the castle itself. This enabled some cargo destined for the castle to be carried directly to the castle, again avoiding Steyning's port fees. When one walks eastward down the moat path from the bridge, one finds that that there is a place where a kind of stairway formerly existed, and it leads right down to where that old channel was dug. If there were no moat, this path up to the castle would not have been possible, due to the steepness of the way. The pathway to the channel presumes the moat, and vice versa.

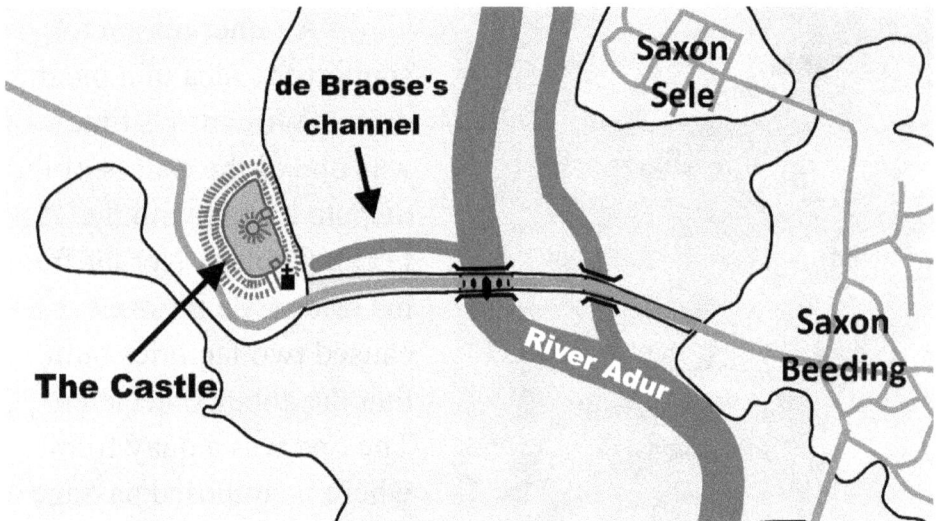

As written earlier, it is certainly possible that King John had the moat deepened after taking custody of the castle in 1211. This would have been about 140 years after the construction of the castle – and the deepening may indeed have contributed to the later instability that seems to have caused the collapse of the gate tower.

The current village of Bramber is about 300 feet wide along The Street, taking into account the gardens and parking areas on either side of the drainages which still exist to help prevent flooding. But when examining Ordnance Survey maps one notices that most of Bramber is currently less than 5 meters above mean sea level! Obviously, even with all the material used to raise the causeway, much settling over the mud flats has occurred. It's clear that the village could easily be flooded if the embankments of the River Adur were to fail at high tide.

In fact, this has happened in both the ancient and the recent past, when high spring tides corresponded with heavy rainfall, raising the river's level well above expectations and even overtopping the later flood-control embankments. And according to the current flood warning authority, Bramber is still entirely within the danger area of the proverbial 100-year-flood. Much preventive effort has been taken since the last time this happened, but flooding is still within the realm of possibility.

The last time this approached flood stage was in 2020 during Storm Ciara.

In any case, the founding of Bramber village seems to have occurred as a result of the infilling of the part of the tidal basin crossing over to Beeding village. This would have been sometime between 1071, when the castle was built, and 1086, when contemporary documents mention the bridge in connection with tolls paid to William de Braose for passage up the river.

The Bramber Flood 1924

29 December 1924

6 July 2023

Salt-making in the Adur Estuary

As mentioned briefly above, the one occupation that could be done on the mud flats of the river's estuary was salt-harvesting.

Because of the shallowness of the water close to the shore of an estuary, salt-making could be a useful occupation for many people who lived in such an area. They would use artificially created earthen platforms (called "salterns") which would become small islets during high tide. Workers would scoop the briny sand and water into pans (originally ceramic and later metal), and filter then boil it down to salty dregs. Since the estuary water usually had silt suspended in it, the salt produced using these salterns tended to be brownish in color. The Adur estuary had an especially busy salt-harvesting business and the Domesday Book recorded at least 58 salterns there. There are a number of saltern platforms still visible in the former estuary of the Adur, though most have been destroyed due to agricultural and other activities.

At Upper Beeding, not far from St. Peter Church, there is a location called "Saltings Field" where three saltern platforms have been preserved. There are placards there explaining the salt-making activity, as well as describing the plant and animal life which are found in the area. Due to erosion, the platforms are much shorter now than they would have been when salt-making was still active – the last such activity there is believed to have been in the early 1500s. By then salt-harvesting had become much less profitable due to the silting up of the estuary.

It's important to mention salt-harvesting in connection with de Braose for the simple reason that either he himself had salterns built just south of the castle or took over existing salterns. He then either had his own workmen harvest salt from them, or he rented them to others for the purpose.

Figure 28

William de Braose vs the Monks of Fécamp Abbey

William de Braose became one of the most powerful men in the kingdom. And like any upstanding powerful man in medieval times, he felt quite free to exercise that power! And like any upstanding powerful man in medieval times who exercised his power, occasionally he came into conflict with other upstanding powerful men or organizations.

One such powerful organization was the Benedictine Abbey at Fécamp, Normandy. And it might be worth mentioning that the town of Fécamp was where William the Conqueror's own castle of residence in Normandy was located. And remember that Fécamp Abbey had helped fund and organize the invasion of England. Hence, King William owed the abbey some favors!

So, before setting out on the conquest which gave him England, the Conqueror had sworn to Fécamp that he would restore to the abbey the benefits at Steyning which the English lords Godwin and Harold had taken from them. He even solemnized this promise with an oath sworn on a knife!

Accordingly, upon taking the throne of England, King William did fulfill his oath to the monks of Fécamp and restored their privileges at St. Cuthman's Church in Steyning, along with its associated income-producing benefits.

But it wasn't long before de Braose began to cut into those privileges and benefits enjoyed by Fécamp. The first thing that he did was to start offering burial plots in his St. Nicholas churchyard. As consecrated ground, every good Christian would want to be buried in a hallowed spot, rather than with the heathens! Of course, nothing is truly free, and so burial in hallowed ground would involve the payment of a fee, and no doubt de Braose offered his burial space at a discount from Fecamp's fee for burial at St. Cuthman's Church in Steyning. The monks objected to this, because St. Nicholas had been built to serve the castle and not the town, yet here was de Braose luring their customers away!

De Braose had also begun to use land the Abbey considered theirs for the creation of burgage[18] plots near Steyning, which were then rented to common folk for farming. Before he was done, there were 18 such plots being rented out. Other encroachments on Abbey lands and privileges included salt harvesting, a farmed rabbit warren, and a hunting park near Odiham in Hampshire. Some salt harvesting activity was taking place in the marshland just south of the castle that was nominally part of Fécamp's manor land.

One final issue, a channel diverting river water to the castle that was mentioned earlier, was seen as a serious potential problem due to the Adur estuary silting up over time. There was a concern that this channel would reduce the flow of water up to Steyning's port. This was a theoretical threat to the viability of Steyning's port, and therefore a threat to Fécamp's substantial income from it, in addition to the aforementioned quay and tollhouse near the new bridge on the river which was charging passage fees for boats going both up and down river.

Fécamp made frequent complaints about all this to King William, but the king put off any decision about them for many years. Although he owed Fécamp a debt of honor for their

---

[18] A burgage was a town ("borough" or "burgh") rental property, owned by a king or lord. The property, a "burgage tenement," usually consisted of a house on a long and narrow plot of land, with a narrow street frontage. Rental payment was usually in the form of money, but each "burgage tenure" arrangement was unique and could include services.

support during the Conquest, he also owed de Braose a debt of honor for his support not only in the Conquest, but also in conflicts in both England and the Continent. The king was kind of stuck between a rock and the proverbial hard place – not to mention that the king himself was encroaching on Fécamp for strategic reasons, by keeping the income and privileges of similar properties at Hastings, which had been similarly promised to Fécamp!

Matters finally came to a head in 1085 and 1086, when the king decided to put the matter finally to rest. In 1085 he finally confirmed Fécamp's claims regarding Steyning and compensated the abbey for its claims at Hastings with land in the manor of Bury, near Pulborough in Sussex. And in 1086, King William called his sons, barons and bishops to court to settle the Steyning disputes with de Braose. This was the last time an English king presided personally, with his full court, to decide a matter of law. The matter took a full day, and the result was a complete judgement in the abbey's favor.

What this meant to de Braose was that he was forced to curtail his quay tolls, to give up his various encroachments onto the abbey's lands, burgages, rabbit warrens, salterns, and that park in Odiham, and he had to fill up the channel he had used to divert the river to his moat. Finally, he had to organize a mass exhumation of all the dead buried at Saint Nicholas's church at Bramber and have them transferred to the abbey's churchyard of Saint Cuthman's in Steyning. Of course, this would have included the transfer of burial fees to the abbey as well.

All of this would have been a blow to William's income, but since he had profited by these and other measures for a couple of decades, and he still had plenty of other sources of income, as well as being extremely wealthy, the setback wouldn't have put his affairs into too large a crimp.

The secular canons established by de Braose at the St. Peter church in Beeding are long gone, the priory having been dissolved when King Henry VIII took over all monastic properties at the time the Church of England was established. The priory building at Sele in Upper Beeding no longer exists, but in its place is a private house built in the late 18th century as the parish's vicar's residence. It was probably built using some of the materials left over from the priory. This building, called The Priory, is now a private residence, and is not associated with the church.

Figure 29 - Aerial view of St. Peters and The Priory

Civil War

In 1087, William the Conqueror died. He had wanted his two older sons, Robert Curthose and William Rufus[19], to split his domains between them. His last will and testament stated that the Dukedom of Normandy should go to Robert, and the Kingdom of England should go to William II. William I's third son, Henry, was not overlooked in his father's will, but he received no title of nobility, and inherited only a token amount of estate land (which his brother William refused to give him) and a sum of money.

This dividing of inheritances between William and Robert did not sit well with the Norman barons, since many of them held estates in both Normandy and England, and with their loyalties being divided like this, they foresaw serious problems. Neither were Robert and William II very happy not to be given *both* Normandy and England. The resulting conflict was a mess and lasted for decades. During all of this the de Braose family sided with William Rufus, who became King William II of England.

Succession

On Sunday, 11 December 1093 William 1 de Braose attended his last known public event, a dedicatory Mass at the new priory of Saint Gervais that he had financed in his home barony in Briouze. As background, William had spent much time, effort, and money to help establish that priory, which, like

---

[19] Rufus was not a surname, but a nickname, used to distinguish him from his father. "Rufus" was Latin for "the Red." This was most likely due to his having red hair.

his priory in Beeding, was subordinate to the Benedictine Abbey of Saint-Florent de Saumur.

William seemed to be concerned for the future of the priory, so much so that he unexpectedly pre-empted the bishop's celebration of the dedicatory Mass to make a public declaration of support, binding his heirs to it. He borrowed a dagger from one of the monks present at the service, and placing it upon the altar, he recited his family gifts to the priory, and forced his son Philip to place his hands on the dagger with him, performing the ceremony commonly called "swearing upon a knife." As the reader may remember, in preparation for his invasion of England, William the Conqueror similarly swore upon a knife to uphold Fécamp Abbey's claims in England.

Nobody knows why, but Philip had apparently been unwilling to confirm the grants his father had made to the priory, and this was William's way of forcing him to do so publicly. This would have made it virtually impossible for Philip to disavow his support privately after his father's demise. We can only assume that Philip had expressed himself in opposition to continuing to support the priory, against his father's wishes.

Why a knife? Presumably, this was supposed to signify that only one's death (as by a knife) would prevent fulfillment of the oath. This might sound strange to our modern ears, but it isn't as foreign as you might think! Perhaps you may remember, as a child, having promised something with the words "cross my heart and hope to die, stick a needle in my eye"? Well, surprise! This kind of swearing you did as a child has an ancient origin!

This was the last time William de Braose, the First Lord of Bramber, appears in the public record. The next time an act

71

of the Lord of Bramber was recorded, it was in 1096, and the name attached to the Lordship was that of his son Philip.

When, where, and how did William die? There's no record of his death, though some have speculated that he may have died in battle in Normandy sometime during the dispute between Duke Robert and King William II. Given that at his probable date of death he would have been between 56 and 66 years old, it seems unlikely that he would have been actively engaged in combat. It is more probable that he died of causes incident to old age, or illness. For William's year of death, I've split the difference and called it 1094.

Philip I de Braose

2nd Lord of Bramber

Life: ??? – 1134
Tenure: 1094 – 1134

At William de Braose's death, Philip de Braose inherited his father's titles and lands. Like his father, he favored the side of King William II against Duke Robert, and with that king he helped to extend the Norman Conquest into parts of Wales.

In 1097 at the king's behest, and in concert with him, Philip led forces into the Welsh county of Powys, and though these expeditions were not particularly successful overall, Philip was able to take and hold lands around the towns of Builth and Radnor. He had a motte-and-bailey castle built at Builth and might also have done so at Radnor as well, though the site some have identified at Radnor as Philip's may not have been a fortification at all. The castle at Builth was a classic wood fortification that ended up changing hands between Normans and the Welsh over the next hundred years, until Edward I ("Longshanks") built a large stone structure there.

All that remains of the castle at Builth today is just the earthworks. All the stone has been robbed away over the centuries for use in other buildings.

In 1100, just a few years after the death of Philip's father, King William II died without an heir. The previously disregarded fourth son of the Conqueror, Henry, who had originally been bought off with a large sum of money and a pittance of land (that William II actually confiscated before he got it), now came in and took the throne of England, becoming

King Henry I. Philip de Braose quickly gave the new king his full support.

Philip's support of Henry I earned him great favor with the king, and once Henry's rule over England was secure, it appears that Philip took advantage of the still uneasy peace to go on Crusade to the Holy Land for a time, which he did in 1103.

In 1110, sometime after he returned from Crusade, and for unknown reasons Philip rebelled against King Henry I, and as a result the king confiscated all his estates. Fortunately, after two years the king forgave him and gave it all back. We can only speculate on the causes for both events!

Philip was a very rich man; it is said that during his life he was the tenth wealthiest layman in England. Besides his conquests in Wales, and all that he had inherited from his father, Philip also ended up in control of half of his father-in-law's estates, when those estates passed to his wife's ownership.

Family

Philip married Aenor de Totnes, who was one the two daughters of Juhel de Totnes, the feudal baron of Totnes and of Barnstaple, both in Devon. Because Juhel died without male heirs, Philip acquired half of the property of the feudal barony of Barnstaple, which he received in right of his wife.

Philip and Aenor had two sons and two daughters that we know about. These were:

- William 2 de Braose, Philip's eldest son and heir, who became the 3rd Lord of Bramber upon Philip's death.

- Philip 2 de Braose, Philip 1's second son, who was an unsuccessful adventurer.
- Their two daughters were named Basilia and Gillian.

Last Acts

Apparently, Philip suffered from blindness towards the end of his life. The story of how he became blind is rather dramatic, since it was attributed to divine disfavor and not to any physical accident or illness.

The story goes that sometime during the reign of Henry I, while he was visiting Builth, he took his dogs out hunting. Upon the close of day he found that he was near the church of St. Afan, and decided to spend the night in the church rather than return to his castle in the darkness. At first light the next day Philip woke to find that not only had all his dogs had gone mad, he himself was blind! This was seen as punishment for having disrespected the sanctity of the church.

From then on Philip lived in darkness, but after some time decided to redeem himself for his supposed offense against God. According to this story, in 1130 he handed over the governance of his lands to his son, William 2, and later, with the help of loyal companions traveled to the Holy Land. His friends took him to the front line of battle on his war horse, where he charged the enemy, sightless but with sword in hand, and so met an honorable death.

Whether this story or any part of it is true or not, Philip had certainly departed this life sometime between 1137 and 1139.

William 2 de Braose

3rd Lord of Bramber

Life: ??? – 1179?
Tenure: 1139 – 1179?

When Philip de Braose's son William became the Lord of Bramber he was already one of the richest men in England, and by the end of his life he had increased this wealth substantially. He owned or controlled a number of estates in Normandy, as well as in Sussex, Dorset, Devon and Gloucestershire in England, and Brecon, Abergavenny, Builth and New Radnor in Wales.

Besides being very rich in property and income, William 2 acquired influence and power as an important player in English politics during his tenure as Lord of Bramber.

After King Henry I died without a legitimate male successor, William 2 was a supporter of Stephen de Blois's claim to the throne, in opposition to Henry I's daughter Matilda, whom King Henry had declared his successor. The dispute between Stephen and Matilda led to an 18-year long armed dispute, a civil war known as *The Anarchy*, and by the time it ended in 1153, William had shifted his loyalty to Matilda's son, Henry of Anjou. In the end, Stephen was forced to sign an agreement allowing him to continue as King, but his two sons were passed over for the crown in favor of this Henry, who a year later became Henry II upon Stephen's death. Henry was the first Plantagenet king and is possibly best recognizable as the king in the 1968 film "The Lion in Winter", played by Peter O'Toole.

Lord William spent a great deal of time working with King Henry II, going on campaign and various expeditions throughout the king's realms, including in France and Ireland. When the king faced rebellion by his sons (if you've seen the aforementioned film, you can appreciate the complexity of the situation), William was entrusted with maintaining the king's interests in Herefordshire, being appointed as the shire reeve, or Sheriff.

Family

William 2 and his wife, Bertha of Hereford, had 2 sons and 2 daughters:
- William 3 de Braose, 4th Lord of Bramber
- Roger
- Sibyl
- Maud

Succession

Until 1175, the de Braose family had been in the good graces of King Henry II, but one act of William 2's son, William 3, caused this favor to temporarily evaporate. This was the massacre at Abergevenny of a number of Welsh lords and princes. More about this below.

William 2 died in 1179, and his lordship passed to his eldest son, William 3.

William 3 de Braose

4th Lord of Bramber[20]

Life: 1153? – 1211
Tenure: 1179 – 1211

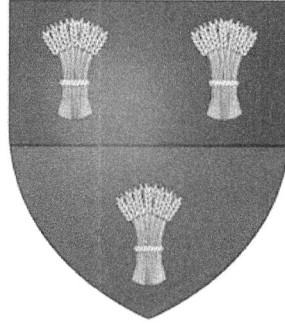

William 3 de Braose was the 4th Lord of Bramber, a court favorite of King John of England, and was, at the peak of his power, also Lord of Gower, Abergavenny, Brecknock, Builth, Radnor, Kington, Limerick, Glamorgan, Skenfrith, Grosmont, White Castle, and Briouze in Normandy. William 3's tenure as Lord of Bramber marked the height of power of the House of Braose, for all that it started under a cloud of royal disapproval. This disapproval was due to his actions pertaining to the Welsh leaders he betrayed in the Abergevenny Massacre and its aftermath.

---

[20] Arms attributed to William 3 de Braose (d.1211) by Matthew Paris in *Historia Anglorum, Chronica Majora, Part III* (1250–59) British Library MS Royal 14 C VII f. 29v[6]: Party per fesse gules and azure, three garbs or. Authenticity of these arms is considered doubtful. – this version licensed under Creative Commons by Deed v3, unattributed.

The Ogre of Abergavenny

The one thing that is certain about the Abergavenny Massacre is that William 3 de Braose invited Seisyll[21] ap[22] Dyfnwal, Seisyll's son Geoffrey, and several other Welsh lords to a dinner at Abergavenny Castle sometime around Christmas 1175, and then treacherously murdered them all in cold blood.

From there, the causes and the aftermaths become very clouded because of contradictory stories and a puzzling lack of precision as to places and dates.

As to causes, the least reliable tale is from one contemporary source, Gerald of Wales. Gerald claimed that King Henry II was getting very annoyed over the constant rebellions by Welsh lords and princes, so he issued orders that all Welshmen were to be forbidden to possess weapons. In pursuance of this order, in 1175 William 3 supposedly invited several Welsh lords and princes to a Christmas dinner at Abergevenny Castle, where he announced this new policy. They objected strenuously, and William was forced to have his men kill them all, allegedly in self-defense.

It's very well known that Gerald of Wales was a de Braose partisan, and his version of events is patently ridiculous. In the first place, A policy of disarmament would have been unenforceable, and secondly, as far as this writer has been able to find, no such order was ever issued by King Henry.

---

[21] The Welsh name Seisyll is commonly anglicized to "Cecil".

[22] Welsh names, especially those of noble families, like the Normano-English, did not have surnames, as such, but used patronymics, by which children were identified as to who their father was. In the Welsh language "ap" meant "son of" and "ferch" meant "daughter of." In the case of Seisyll, he was "son of Dyfnwal".

More likely, the immediate motive for what William did had to do with the murder of his uncle, Henry FitzMiles, the brother of his mother Bertha.

It isn't known for certain who killed FitzMiles, but the man who was most immediately suspected was Seisyll ap Dyfnwal, who was the Lord of Upper Gwent. Two locations are mentioned when the event is recounted, namely Seisyll's Castle Arnault and Henry's own castle at Abergavenny. When the murder took place is likewise full of uncertainty – dates from between 1159 and 1163 but even as late as 1175 are mentioned. Since Fitzmiles was appointed Baron of Abergavenny in 1160, it seems unlikely that his murder was earlier than this.

Was Seisyll the actual villain? Nobody really seems to know, and de Braose was apparently determined to get revenge on every Welsh leader who *could* have done it. So, under the pretense of reconciliation after what had been a period of conflict, De Braose invited Seisyll and his son Geoffrey to his castle at Abergavenny for a Christmas feast in 1175[23], along with other Welsh leaders from Gwent. Not all of those invited accepted the invitation, because they quite frankly did not trust de Braose's offer of reconciliation.

One part of Gerald of Wales very skewed version of events does have a backhanded ring of truth in it when he wrote of disarmament. It was simply that William's invited guests did politely surrender their weapons upon entrance to the castle, trusting that he was sincere in his claims of peace. And thus, they were unarmed and unable to defend themselves when William's men at arms attacked them during the dinner in his Great Hall.

---

[23] De Braose had inherited this castle from his uncle at his uncle's death.

One might see a certain degree of justice in avenging oneself upon one who had killed a family member. Even if the culpability was not quite certain, for in those days determination of guilt was in cases without witnesses extremely primitive and uncertain in their efficacy. But to kill not only the chief suspect, but the suspect's eldest son? And the suspect's companions? And while these men were invited guests at a dinner advertised to be for reconciliation? One would have to conclude that this was murder most foul. But de Braose didn't stop there.

The massacre seems most likely to be a ploy to remove not only Seisyll but also his potential supporters, as can be seen by his actions after the massacre, when he and his men rode to Seisyll's home where they murdered Seisyll's 7-year-old son, Cadwaladr, either took his mother captive or killed her, and then ravaged Seisyll's lands. Not even stopping there, de Braose and his men hunted down the men who had been invited to the dinner but who had refused to come and despoiled and seized all of their lands as well.

This horrendous and treacherous act earned for William 3 the nickname among the Welsh the "Ogre of Abergavenny", and for generations afterwards the de Braose family was regarded with great hostility by many Welsh. Additionally, because of the disrepute it had brought to English-Welsh relations, it caused King Henry II to withdraw his favor from the de Braose family. It was probably for this reason that William 3's father retired to his estates, largely withdrawing from public life, until his death 4 years later.

A later consequence occurred in 1182, when Hywel ap Iorwerth, lord of Caerleon, in retribution for Seisyll's murder ordered the destruction of Dingestow Castle, a de Braose property then under construction, and had Abergavenny Castle set afire. These attacks were carried out by Seisyll's remaining relatives and their supporters. De Braose was not at the castle when it was burnt, but many of de Braose's men who were present and not killed in the attack were taken hostage.

Restoration of Favor

After the ascension of King Henry II's son Richard I Lionheart to the throne in 1189, William 3's loyal support of Richard caused his family to be restored eventually to the good graces of the royal family. And when Richard I was killed in battle in 1199, William's immediate support of Prince John's bid for the throne earned him great rewards from John, including lordship over a number of rich provinces in Ireland and Wales, making him one of the most powerful barons in the kingdom. This rise in power was remarkable, and garnered William a good degree of jealousy from the other barons.

William 3 was described by Sidney Painter as follows:

"Perhaps the most interesting as well as the most powerful baron in this group [of early supporters of John] was William de Briouse... William was extremely rapacious and high in John's favor. During the early years of John's reign he was to use the king's benevolence, ancient claims, and pure conquest to increase his lands greatly."

The Disappearance of Arthur I, Duke of Brittany

This rapid rise in power and wealth also earned William suspicion regarding his involvement in the mysterious

82

disappearance of King John's nephew, Arthur, Duke of Brittany, who was a possible competitor for the English throne and the Dukedom of Normandy. Were all those lordships that King John gave to de Braose a reward for the act or was it perhaps a bribe to keep silence over Arthur's fate? That was a rumor that was "in the wind" at the time.

It might be a good time to ask who was this Arthur, Duke of Brittany, and why was he a threat to John's power? It comes down to the system of royal inheritance that was in effect all the way up to modern times, when the first significant change in a millennium occurred.

King Henry II had four legitimate sons who lived to adulthood, and in order by birth they were:

- Henry, aka "the Young King"
- Richard, aka "the Lionheart"
- Geoffrey
- John, aka "Lackland"

Henry the Young King would have been king upon the death of his father, but he died 6 years before, making Richard the next in line for the throne. Geoffrey died 3 years before his father, but not before fathering a son, who was named Arthur. Richard Lionheart ascended the throne when Henry II died in 1189, but he had no legitimate children. When he died in 1199, his brother John took the throne.

John's ascension to the throne was actually more complex than that. However, this book is about the de Braose family, and so we must leave aside most of the very complex behind-the-scenes wheeling and dealing between the two sides of the issue. Under the system of male primogeniture John was not necessarily entitled to the throne, for although he was the eldest surviving son of King Richard's predecessor, Henry II, there was yet another descendant of Henry, who was John's deceased elder brother Geoffrey's young son Arthur. So, Arthur was actually senior to John in the line of succession as it was understood.

On his deathbed, however, King Richard had supposedly declared to his barons who were present and to his mother, Queen Eleanor, that John should succeed him. One of those barons was William 3 de Braose, and it appears that he was the prime supporter of John. In any event, it became a question of who had the strongest army.

John was supported by the bulk of the English and Norman nobility and was crowned at Westminster. On the other hand, Arthur was supported by the majority of the Breton, Maine and Anjou nobles on the continent, and received the support of King Philip II of France as well. And thus, a rebellion began.

The final outcome of the rebellion was that John lost Normandy to Phillip of France but kept his English throne. Before the loss of Normandy, it happened that John's forces won a battle at Mirebeau in 1202, and captured his nephew and competitor for the throne, young Arthur, the Duke of Brittany. Arthur was kept confined for a time, but then he disappeared under mysterious circumstances, and no-one knew what happened to him[24].

---

[24] Arthur had a younger sister named Eleanor (1182-1241), reputed to be quite beautiful, whose fate was less dark. She was kept as a royal prisoner for the rest of her life, being forbidden to marry and confined in various castles, but provided with a comfortable living including servants. Under Salic law, she was eligible to become Queen regnant in her own right, and was thus a danger to the reign of both John and his heir, Henry III. They were rather apologetic about it, for what it was worth – i.e. not much.

This is where suspicion falls upon William 3 de Braose. During the Battle of Mirabeau in 1203, our William was the one who personally captured young Arthur, who was 13 years old at the time. And since William was a loyal supporter of King John the king entrusted him with custody over Arthur. It was during this time that Arthur vanished and was presumably murdered. Some remembered how the Welsh leaders were murdered at Abergevenny and wondered if William had been responsible for Arthur's death as well. There is no evidence for this, but there was some talk about how King John tried to get some of his other followers to do away with Arthur, but Arthur's youthful innocence so prevailed upon them that no-one would do it, so John killed Arthur himself, and had his body dumped into the River Seine. In any case, no one now knows what happened – and Arthur was never seen again.

It seems certain that William de Braose was aware of what the King had done, since it was done while Arthur was in his custody. As to whether William did the deed, that seems unlikely, given what followed.

Royal Persecution and Death in Exile

The matter of Arthur and William de Braose might have ended there, with a dark rumor, and King John endowing William with additional properties and gifts, ostensibly buying his silence.

But in 1208, a quarrel developed between William de Braose and his friend and patron King John. It's not known precisely why this was, but on the surface, it was because William owed the King a large sum of money, 5,000 marks. But John's actions went far beyond what would be necessary to ensure William's eventual repayment of the debt. One story which has come down to us is that John sent some of his officers to demand that William hand over his son, William[25], to be a hostage for William's loyalty, and the repayment of the debt.

Upon the demand being made, it is said that William's wife Maud refused to allow it, stating loudly and in the hearing of the officers that she would not deliver her children to a king who had murdered his own nephew. This remark was reported to the King, and he immediately acted to squelch any further loose talk. Troops were sent to occupy and confiscate all de Braose property, and the family fled.

Maud and her son William 4 briefly sheltered in Ireland with Maud's daughter who was married to an Irish lord, but when that refuge became untenable, they fled and were captured while trying to reach the safety of Scotland.

King John had them imprisoned in 1210 in either Corfe Castle in Devon or Windsor Castle[26], where, as legend has it, they were starved to death by being walled up in the dungeon. William 3 himself finally ended up in Corbeil, France after being pursued by the King's henchmen from England to Ireland, and then Wales. He briefly allied with Welsh prince Llewelyn the Great against King John but died in Corbeil in 1211.

William 3's date of death, 9 August 1211, is the first de Braose for whom we have a definite date of birth or death.

---

[25] William 4 was an adult with at least one son, named John, at the time of his death.

[26] Sources vary on which castle this happened in.

The 20th Century historian Sidney Painter, in his biography of King John, *The Reign of King John*[27], said of this persecution of the de Braose family:

"The quarrel with William de Briouse and his family was the greatest mistake John made during his reign. It should have been avoided at any cost. For one thing it made his cruelty known to all his barons."

Just a few years later, King John's barons forced him to sign the Magna Carta, which put limits on the monarch's powers and helped to form the ethical basis of the future government of England.

Knepp Castle

Although it was William 2, not William 3 who built what is known as Knepp Castle in Sussex, it was during William 3's time that it became noteworthy. This is due to its renovation by King John after he confiscated the de Braose properties.

What is left of the castle is located west of the village of West Grinstead. Like Bramber Castle, Knepp Castle is near the course of the River Adur; in this case, the west branch of the river. William 2 built it according to the usual motte-and-bailey plan, and it would originally have been largely constructed from wood.

The name of the castle, Knepp with a silent "k" in modern English, is believed to derive from the word "cnæpp", an Old English word for top or summit (also "button"), referring to the natural mound upon which the motte of the castle was constructed, after being enlarged by the builders.

---

[27] Published in 1949 by Johns Hopkins University Press. The quoted passage occurs on pages 250-251 of the 1949 edition.

William 2 de Braose is believed to have built this castle primarily as a hunting lodge, with its secondary purpose as a defensive backup to Bramber Castle, in case of coastal danger.

After King John confiscated the former de Braose lands he had many repairs and enhancements made to both Bramber and Knepp Castles.

The king had Knepp castle rebuilt in stone, making it more of a "proper" castle. Eventually the castle came back into the hands of the de Braose family, but after the 14th century this castle was largely allowed to fall into ruin, and by the mid-18th century most of the stone of the castle had been robbed away, leaving just one corner of the keep still standing. The ruin is now owned by the Burrell baronets[28], who built a manor house nearby, also known as Knepp Castle.

Knepp Castle is located 7 miles north of Bramber, near West Grinstead. The remains of the castle are visible to drivers passing by on the A24 highway.

Family

William 3 and his wife, Matilda, aka Maud, are reputed to have had 16 children. The most well-documented are these:

- Matilda (Maud) - married Gruffydd ap Rhys II
- William 4 – died with his mother while imprisoned by King John; he was the father of John de Braose, who became the Lord of Bramber after his two uncles, Giles and Reginald
- Giles – a churchman who became the Bishop of Hereford – he was briefly the 5th Lord of Bramber

---

[28] A "baronet" is a hereditary knight.

- Reginald – 6th Lord of Bramber – he sold the Lordship of Bramber to his nephew, John de Broase, who was the son of William 4 de Braose
- John – eventually the 7th Lord of Bramber, he married Margaret ferch Llewellyn, and received the title Lord of Gower from her father, Llewellyn the Great.
- Flandrina – a churchwoman who became the Abbess of Godstow

THE REMAINS OF KNEPP CASTLE

Figure 30

Giles de Braose

5th Lord of Bramber

Life: ??? – 1215
Tenure: 1213 – 1215

Giles was the second son of William 3 de Braose, and he took holy orders and became a priest of the Catholic Church. He rose in the hierarchy of the church until 1200 CE, when he was appointed the Bishop of Hereford.

In April or May of 1208, at about the start of the trouble between his father William 3 and King John, Giles seems to have briefly been put into custody as a hostage for his father's good behavior, but by June 1208 he had escaped to France, where he joined other English exiles in conspiring against King John. One of the efforts to which he was party was assisting Llywelyn the Great, King of Gwynedd (and the virtual ruler of Wales), to make an alliance with French King Phillip II.

Possibly in order to reduce the count of enemies working against him, King John allowed Giles to return to England in 1213, and even restored some of the de Braose lands to him. But his efforts to get the King to return lands to his nephew, John, the grandson of William 3, failed, and Giles re-joined the barons opposing the King. In 1214 there was a brief reconciliation between Giles and the barons and King John, but when Llywelyn the Great revolted against the King, Giles and his brother Reginald took advantage of the situation to retake their ancestral lands.

When King John was forced by his other rebellious barons to sign the Magna Carta in June 1215, neither Giles nor his brother Reginald were present, because they refused to compromise with the King.

In October 1215 Giles and King John were again reconciled, and Giles had regained control of his father's lands after paying a fine to the King. Again, he unsuccessfully attempted to have the king give his nephew John the lordship. Giles died on 17 November 1215 in Worcester and was buried in Hereford Cathedral. A statue of him still stands on the face of the cathedral.

As a churchman with vows of celibacy, Giles never married and had no children.

Reginald de Braose

6th Lord of Bramber[29]

Life: ??? - 1228
Tenure: 1216 – 1228

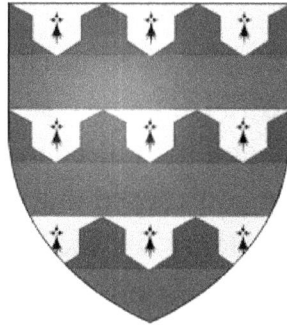

During all the machinations between King John and Reginald's older brother Giles, whereas Giles had been reconciled with and alienated from the King a number of times, Reginald was apparently too deeply angry with the King, because he remained at odds with him.

However, after Giles' death in November 1215, King John finally acquiesced to Reginald's claims to the de Braose estates in Wales in May 1216. Reginald thus became Lord of Brecon, Abergavenny, and Builth, some of which had been previous de Braose Lordships in the Welsh marches. There was still the potential of conflict, however, since Reginald was also very much a vassal of the Welsh leader Llewelyn the Great, Prince of Gwynedd, who had become his father-in-law in 1215 when Reginald married Llywelyn's daughter, Gwladus Ddu.

---

[29] Arms of Giles de Braose (d.1215) and his brother Reginald de Braose (d.1228), younger sons of William III de Braose (d.1211) : "Barry of six vair gules and ermine and azure" – this version licensed under Creative Commons by Deed v3 by Jaspe

After King John's death in 1216, in 1217 his successor Henry III restored Reginald to royal favor and lordship over the many of the former de Braose properties, including the Bramber lordship and estates. Rather than keeping Bramber for himself, Reginald sold the lordship of Bramber to his nephew, John, in 1226.

Because of King Henry's restoration of the de Braose estates in 1217, there was a great deal of turmoil between Reginald and his father-in-law, Llewelyn, probably because Llewelyn considered that Reginald was beholden to both him and King Henry for some of the same properties, thus dividing his loyalty. This led to intermittent fighting between them, and in 1228, Reginald's son William by his first wife, Graecia Brewer, was captured and held for ransom by Llewelyn. The demanded ransom was an alliance, a sum of money, and a promise to marry William's daughter Isabella to Llywelyn's son Dafydd.

Reginald died sometime around 1228, leaving William 5 as the heir to Reginald's various Welsh lordships. But after the alliance between William and Llywelyn had been agreed to, it was discovered that while William had been a prisoner of Llywelyn, he had committed adultery with Llywelyn's wife, Joan![30] Upon this discovery Llywelyn had William re-captured and subsequently executed by hanging in 1230. The marriage between their two children still took place, however.

Shortly after the hanging, Prince Llywelyn wrote to William's widow Eva, offering his apologies, telling her that he had been forced to order the hanging upon insistence by his

---

[30] Joan was an illegitimate daughter of King John, later legitimated by the Pope.

Welsh lords. He concluded by adding that he hoped the execution would not affect their business dealings!

Because of his sinful behavior with Joan, and the general dislike for the de Braose family in general, this William was known as *Gwilym Ddu* or "Black William" among the Welsh. Because William had four daughters but no sons, his estates were divided between his daughters[31], and his titles were inherited by his cousin, John de Braose.

---

[31] This would have taken place after William's wife Eva's death, as she continued to hold those estates in her own right after her husband's execution.

John de Braose

7ᵗʰ Lord of Bramber

Life: 1197 – 1232
Tenure: 1226 – 1232

Born in 1197, John was the eldest grandson of William 3 de Braose, whose wife Maud had apparently triggered King John's seizure of all de Braose lands. His father, William 4, died when John was about 12 years old. Due to this unhappy event he was given the nickname "Tadody" by the Welsh. This word means "fatherless" in the Welsh language.

After his father's death, John was hidden for some time in his family's estates in Gower, Wales, until he was given into the care of his uncle, Giles. But in 1214 he was captured by the king and held in custody until 1216 when the king died. It wasn't until 1218 that he was released by King John's heir, Henry III.

In 1219 he married Margaret ferch Llywelyn, daughter of the leader of Wales, Llywelyn Fawr (also known as Llywelyn the Great). He received the Lordship of Gower as her dowry with Llywelyn's blessing. This was a former de Braose lordship in any case.

According to most understandings of the principle of male primogeniture, he should have been the lawful heir of the de Braose line, being the eldest son of the eldest son, but circumstances had not favored it until his uncle Reginald sold him the honor of Bramber in 1226.

95

Upon Reginald's son William's death in 1228, John inherited the Welsh lordships of Brecon, Abergavenny, and Builth.

He didn't possess these for very long, however, because he died by accident just four years later at the young age of 34, when he fell from his horse while riding around his land in Bramber on 18 July 1232. His lands and titles passed to his son, William 6.

William 6 de Braose

8th Lord of Bramber, 1st Baron Braose[32]

Life: 1224 – 1291
Tenure: 1232 – 1291

The first de Braose heir to enjoy a long life without significant upheaval in three generations, William 6 inherited the honor of Bramber and most of the traditional de Braose properties upon the death of his father John. Being just 12 years old at the time of his ascension, he would have remained a ward of his mother until around 1245, when he came of age.

He served as a loyal adviser and supporter to both King Henry III and Edward I Longshanks. He sided with King Henry against Simon de Montfort during the civil war in England in the later part of Henry's reign, and when he died in 1291 at age 67, his tenure as Lord of Bramber for 59 years was the longest of any of the de Braose line.

In 1290 William was summoned to sit in Parliament, and this writ of summons created him a Baron, making him the First Baron Braose. He died in the next year, on 5 January 1291 in

---

[32] Arms attributed to William de Breouse in the Camden Roll, ca 1280, blazoned there as "de azur od un leun rampant de or crusile d'or" – this version licensed under Creative Commons by Deed v3 by AlexD

the village of Findon, and was buried in the Priory churchyard at Sele.

Family

William 6 married three times, firstly with Aline, daughter of Thomas de Multon. His second was Agnes, daughter of Nicholas de Moeles. His third wife was Mary, daughter of Robert de Ros.

Children
- with Aline: William 7, who succeeded him as 2nd Baron Braose
- with Agnes: Sir Giles de Braose
- with Mary: Richard, Peter, and Margaret

There may have been other children, but this is uncertain.

William 7 de Braose

9th Lord of Bramber, 2nd Baron Braose[33]

Life: 1260 – 1326
Tenure: 1291 – 1326

William 7 inherited the de Braose lordship and barony upon the death of his father William in 1291.

Although his father's long tenure as Lord of Bramber was not as filled with intrigue and trouble as the previous three generations had been, there was a period of rebellion by many of the barons, led by the Earl of Leicester, Simon de Montfort. Because his father William 6 had supported King Henry III against the rebels, young William 7 was captured by the rebels when he was about 4 years old and held as a hostage for a while in the custody of Montfort's wife, Eleanor. Ironically, Eleanor was King John's youngest daughter.

William 7 continued to be just as strong a supporter of King Henry III and his son Edward I as his father had been and contributed both money and personal military service in Edward's wars in Wales, Scotland, France, and Flanders.

---

[33] Arms of William de Braose as blazoned in the Falkirk Roll of Arms, c. 1298, which gives the tail as doubled: "Azure crusilly (i.e. semy) of crosses crosslet a lion double queued rampant or" – this version licensed under Creative Commons by Deed v3 by AlexD

From 1298 to 1306 he was involved in the Scottish wars, and fought at the Battle of Falkirk on 22 July 1298, when William Wallace (Braveheart) was defeated.

He died in 1326 aged 66 years. He was known as being unable to manage his cash flow well, and was often in debt Thomas Walsingham, an English chronicler (died 1422), stated in one of his chronicles that Braose was "very rich by descent but a dissipater of the property left to him".

Family

William 7 married twice. Firstly with Agnes (of unknown family), and secondly with Elizabeth, the daughter of Raymund de Sully.

Children

- with Agnes: William 8, who would have succeeded him as 3rd Baron Braose, but he appears to have died before his father; and two daughters, Aline and Joan.
- with Elizabeth: No children

William 8 was mentioned in connection with military service in 1311, but when the estate was settled there was no mention of him, and so one must conclude that he had died in the meantime.

Upon the death of William 7 with no living male issue, the lordship of Bramber and the Barony of Braose became extinct. His two daughters, Aline and Joan, each inherited a share of their father's estates, which were then added to their respective husband's lands. His Welsh lordships would also have become extinct.

Aline and Joan de Braose

Aline's father, William 7, had acted as the ward of John de Mowbray, son of the deceased Baron Mowbray, from age 11 until his majority. Part of the attraction for acting in this capacity was that in administering the estates of his ward he would also profit from them. William 7 also used this opportunity to arrange for his daughter Aline to be betrothed to young John.

John de Mowbray and Aline were subsequently married. When William 7 died without male heirs, Aline inherited half of his estates, including Bramber Castle

William 6's other daughter, Joan, who had married James de Bohun, inherited the other half of the Braose estates.

Once Bramber Castle left the possession of the de Braose family in 1326 with the death of the last Baron Braose, first the de Mowbray and later the Howard families took ownership of the castle, both by marriage. Neither family took any pains to maintain the castle, having no need of it, and so it gradually fell into a dilapidated condition, with stone being robbed away by locals who felt they had better uses for it. The grounds were typically used by the local residents as a sort of commons, where cattle were allowed to graze, and various other uses were put to it, including as a place for fetes and parties.

The principals of the Howard family eventually became the Dukes of Norfolk.

The castle, in pretty much the dilapidated condition we find it in today, was sold by the Duke of Norfolk to an entrepreneur in the early 20th century.

The present Duke of Norfolk, as of 2024, whose seat is Arundel Castle in Sussex, is Edward William Fitzalan-Howard,

18th Duke of Norfolk. He is a descendant of the de Braose family through Aline de Braose, daughter of the 9th and final Lord of Bramber.

In 1946 the castle came into the ownership of the National Trust.

Other de Braoses

Research shows that at the time William 7 died in 1326 he had a second cousin, Baron Sir John de Brewes of Stinton, who was a direct male-line descendant of John de Braose, William's great-grandfather. According to male primogeniture, the prevailing law of inheritance at the time, this second cousin could have inherited the Braose Barony. But their ancestry had diverged about 100 years previously, and certainly neither one knew that the other existed.

Even so, that remaining branch of the de Braose family died out in the male line in 1424, so the Braose barony would have become extinct eventually anyway. There might have been a couple of other possible de Braose branches that could have carried on the barony, and interestingly, there was a second creation of the de Braose baronage in 1302 when a Thomas de Braose was raised to the peerage by King Edward I "Longshanks". It seems certain that this Thomas de Braose was a descendant of the original de Braose line, but tracing how they were related has proven unsuccessful. In any event, they never had anything to do with Bramber Castle or with any traditional de Braose holdings, and that baronage went extinct, too, in 1399.

Archaeology

Bramber Castle has been archaeologically investigated once in the 19th and a number of times in both the 20th and 21st centuries. The author is aware of three "digs," in 1908, 1927, and 1966/67;

The 1908 dig was occasioned by excavation of a building foundation, where the remains of possible outer wards were uncovered south of the St. Nicholas church. Unfortunately, I've been unable to find site maps for this.

The 1927 dig was occasioned by road construction near the former Bramber train station where there is now a roundabout on the Steyning Bypass, A283. It found traces of outer wards, as well as some artifacts dating to the period of the castle's construction.

The 1966/67 investigation was far more extensive than the previous digs, but was still of a somewhat limited character, as it was a "training dig." It concentrated on the castle itself, rather than structures and features outside it. The report of this investigation occupies nearly 60 pages in *The Archaelogical Journal*, Volume 134 for 1977.

In 1987 there was a non-invasive examination of the castle's inner bailey which was looking for underground structures (such as building foundations) using gravimeter and magnetometer instruments. It did discover footings of many structures, which were detected in many cases as shallow as half a meter under ground.

Another geophysical survey was undertaken in 2010 over the entirety of the bailey, and largely confirmed the results of the 1987 survey, with more details discovered. The report of this survey suggested that it might be of value to do a proper archaeological investigation of the castle grounds.

A very useful summary of the archaeology of the Bramber area, including the castle and its history is the Historic Character Assessment Report published in August 2004 by the Sussex Extensive Urban Survey (EUS), written by Mr. Roland B. Harris. This is available online.

On the pages following are some details about the geophysical survey in 2010. The report included evidence of ferrous (iron-containing) magnetic anomalies, such as piping. This is interesting, given that in a closer examination of the bridge stonework I discovered a protruding capped-off metal pipe!

In more modern history, the castle grounds were used as a kind of amusement park, and included such features as a tea room and a model steam train that ran around inside the bailey. The pipe I found would possibly have been used to provide running water for the tea room. On the other hand, it might be more recent, for supplying water to the soldiers who manned the pillboxes during the war.

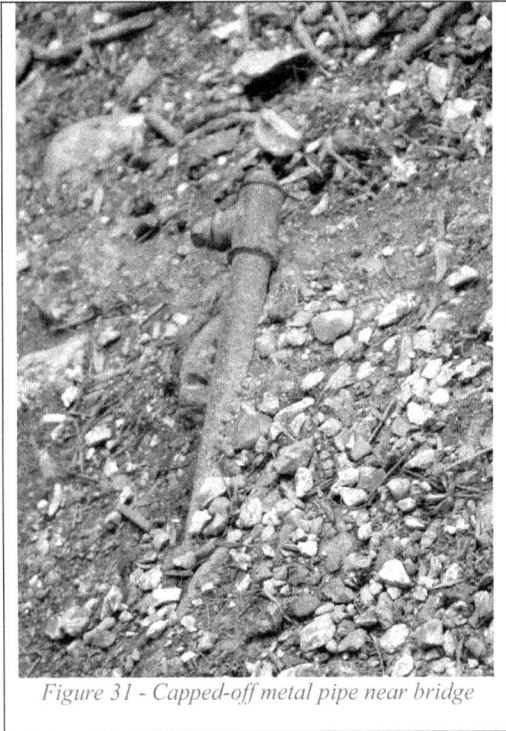

Figure 31 - Capped-off metal pipe near bridge

The report concludes:

"The resistance survey has identified rectilinear outlines of a kind which must represent reasonably intact structural remains in the northern half of the bailey... There may be another less clearly defined structure to the west of the motte...

"It is difficult to determine whether any medieval wall footings survive in the southwest quadrant of the bailey given the disturbed response in the vicinity of the tearoom, and other former structures in this area.

"A structure appears to have been detected to the north of the gatehouse ... , but there is no clear evidence for a cobbled road continuing to the north from the original entrance.

"There may be a fragmentary resistance response to the outer edge of the ditch around the motte ... , but the ditch has not otherwise been detected."

According to the conclusion, there may not be much in the way of archaeological findings possible in the southwest corner of the site due to modern interference in the late 19th and early 20th century. But it is clear that there is still much to learn about the castle. Let us hope that the future will permit such exploration!

www.ingramcontent.com/pod-product-compliance
Lightning Source LLC
Chambersburg PA
CBHW060445040426
42331CB00044B/2648